SCENES FROM THE DRAMA OF EUROPEAN LITERATURE

D0885536

SCENES
FROM THE DRAMA
OF EUROPEAN
LITERATURE

SIX ESSAYS

by Erich Auerbach

Meridian Books, Inc. New York

ERICH AUERBACH

*Erich Auerbach was born in Berlin on November 9, 1892.
Before and after the First World War he studied law,
art history, and philology at leading German universities.
He was professor of romance philology at Marburg
University from 1929 to 1935, when he was discharged by
order of the Nazi regime. Professor Auerbach then
settled in Istanbul, where he taught at the Turkish State
University. He arrived in the United States in 1947,
and held successive posts at Pennsylvania State University,
Princeton's Institute for Advanced Study, and finally
at Yale. Professor Auerbach was the author of several books
—Mimesis is the best-known among them—and many
papers on Italian, French, and medieval Latin literature;
on Christian symbolism and its literary influence;
and on methods of historical criticism. He selected the essays
for the present volume shortly before his death on
October 13, 1957.*

M

A Meridian Books Original Edition
First published by Meridian Books, Inc., April 1959
First printing March 1959

Bibliographical Note

"FIGURA": Translated by Ralph Manheim from the original German text in *Neue Dantestudien* (Istanbul, 1944), pp. 11-71.

ST. FRANCIS OF ASSISI IN DANTE'S "COMMEDIA": Translated by Catherine Garvin from the original German text in *Neue Dantestudien* (Istanbul, 1944), pp. 72-90. This translation first appeared in *Italica*, XXII (December 1945), pp. 166-79.

ON THE POLITICAL THEORY OF PASCAL: Translated by Ralph Manheim from the original German text (with the author's marginal changes) in *Vier Untersuchungen zur Geschichte der französischen Bildung* (Bern, 1951), pp. 51-74. An abridged English translation of this essay, entitled "The Triumph of Evil in Pascal," appeared in *The Hudson Review*, IV (Spring 1951), pp. 58-79.

"LA COUR ET LA VILLE": Translated by Ralph Manheim from the original German text in *Vier Untersuchungen zur Geschichte der französischen Bildung* (Bern, 1951), pp. 12-50.

VICO AND AESTHETIC HISTORISM: Auerbach's own English text, reprinted from *The Journal of Aesthetics and Art Criticism*, VIII (December 1949), pp. 110-18.

THE AESTHETIC DIGNITY OF THE "FLEURS DU MAL": Translated by Ralph Manheim from the original German text in *Vier Untersuchungen zur Geschichte der französischen Bildung* (Bern, 1951), pp. 107-27. An earlier English translation appeared in *The Hopkins Review*, IV (Fall 1950), pp. 29-45.

Contents

"FIGURA"

"FIGURA"

I. From Terence to Quintilian

Originally *figura*, from the same stem as *fingere, figulus, fictor,* and *effigies,* meant "plastic form." Its earliest occurrence is in Terence, who in *Eunuchus* (317) says that a young girl has a *nova figura oris* ("unaccustomed form of face"). The following fragment of Pacuvius (270-1, in Ribbeck, *Scaen. Roman. Poesis Fragm.,* I, 110) probably dates from about the same period:

> *Barbaricam pestem subinis nostris optulit*
> *Nova figura factam . . .*[1]
>
> (To our spears she presented an outlandish plague
> Fashioned in unaccustomed shape.)

The word was probably unknown to Plautus; he twice uses *fictura* (*Trinummus,* 365; *Miles Gloriosus,* 1189); but both times in a sense closer to the activity of forming than to its result; in later authors *fictura* becomes very rare.[2] The mention of *fictura* calls our attention to a peculiarity of *figura:* it is derived directly from the stem and not, like *natura* and other words of like ending, from the supine (Ernout-Meillet, *Dictionnaire étymologique de la langue latine,* 346). An attempt has been made (Stolz-Schmalz, *Lat.*

11

Gramm., 5th edition, 219) to explain this as an as-similation to *effigies:* in any case this peculiar forma-tion expresses something living and dynamic, incom-plete and playful, and it is equally certain that the word had a graceful sound which fascinated many poets. Perhaps it is no more than an accident that in our two oldest examples *figura* occurs in combination with *nova;* but even if accidental, it is significant, for the notion of the new manifestation, the changing as-pect, of the permanent runs through the whole history of the word.

This history begins for us with the Hellenization of Roman education in the last century B.C. Three au-thors played a decisive part in its beginnings: Varro, Lucretius, and Cicero. Of course we can no longer tell exactly what they may have taken over from earlier material that has been lost; but the contributions of Lucretius and Cicero are so distinctive and original that one cannot but credit them with a considerable part in the creation of its meaning.

Varro shows the least originality of the three. If in his writings *figura* sometimes means "outward ap-pearance" or even "outline"[3] and is thus beginning to move away from its earliest signification, the nar-rower concept of plastic form, this seems to have been the result of a general linguistic process, the causes of which we shall discuss further on. In Varro this de-velopment is not even very pronounced. He was an etymologist, well aware of the origin of the word (*fictor cum dicit fingo figuram imponit* ["The image-maker (*fictor*), when he says *fingo* (I shape), puts a *figura* on the thing"]: *De lingua latina*, 6, 78), and thus when he uses the word in connection with living creatures and objects, there is usually a connotation of plastic form. How strong this connotation still was in his time is sometimes hard to decide: for example, when he says that in buying slaves one should consider not only the *figura* but also the qualities—in horses the age, in cocks the breeding value, in apples the aroma (ibid., 9, 35); or when he says that a star has changed its *colorem, magnitudinem, figuram, cursum* (quoted in Augustine, *De civitate Dei,* 21, 8); or when, in *De lingua latina* (5, 117) he compares forked palisade poles with the *figura* of the Latin letter V. The word becomes quite unplastic when he begins to talk of word forms. We have, as he says in *De lingua latina* (9, 21), taken over new forms of vessels from the Greeks; why do people struggle against new word forms, *formae vocabulorum,* as though they were poisonous? *Et tantum inter duos sensus interesse volunt, ut oculis semper aliquas figuras supellectilis novas conquirant, contra auris expertes velint esse?* ("And do they think there is so much difference between the two senses, that they are always looking for new shapes of furniture for their eyes, but yet wish their ears to avoid such things?"). Here we are not far from the idea that figures exist also for the sense of hearing; and it should also be borne in mind that Varro, like all Latin authors who were not specialists in philosophy endowed with an exact terminology, used *figura* and *forma* interchangeably, in the general sense of form. Strictly speaking, *forma* meant "mold," French *"moule,"* and was related to *figura* as the hollow form to the plastic shape that issues from it; but in Varro we seldom find a trace of this distinction, though perhaps we have an exception in the fragment cited in Gellius (III, 10, 7): *semen genitale fit ad capiendam figuram idoneum* ("the life-bearing seed is rendered fit to take on a shape").

As we have intimated, the actual innovation or break with the original meaning, which we first find in Varro, occurs in the field of grammar. It is in

Varro that we first find *figura* used in the sense of
grammatical, inflected, or derived form. In Varro
figura multitudinis means the form of the plural.
Alia nomina quinque habent figuras (9, 52) means:
Some nouns have five case forms. This usage became
widespread (cf. *Thesaurus Linguae Latinae*, VI, s.v.
figura, part 1, III A, 2a, col. 730 and 2e, col. 734);
forma was also much used in the same sense, beginning in Varro's time, but *figura* seems to have been
more popular and frequent with the Latin gram-
marians. How is it possible that both words, but particularly *figura,* the form of which was a clear re-
minder of its origin, should so quickly have taken on
a purely abstract meaning? It happened through the
Hellenization of Roman education. Greek, with its
incomparably richer scientific and rhetorical vocabulary, had a great many words for the concept of form:
morphē, eidos, schēma, typos, plasis, to mention only
the most important. In the philosophical and rhetorical elaboration of the language of Plato and Aristotle,
a special sphere was assigned to each of these words; a
clear dividing line was drawn particularly between
morphē and *eidos* on the one hand and *schēma* on
the other: *morphē* and *eidos* were the form or idea
which "informs" matter; *schēma* is the purely perceptual shape; the classical example of this is Aristotle's *Metaphysics,* VII, 3, 1029a, in which he dis-
cusses *ousia* (essence); here *morphē* is defined as
schēma tēs ideas, the ideal form; thus Aristotle employs *schēma* in a purely perceptual sense to designate
one of the qualitative categories, and he also uses it
in the combinations with *megethos, kinēsis,* and
chrōma that we have already encountered in Varro.
It was only natural that *forma* should come to be used
in Latin for *morphē* and *eidos,* since it originally
conveyed the notion of model; sometimes we also find

exemplar; for *schēma* on the other hand *figura* was usually employed. But since in the learned Greek terminology—in grammar, rhetoric, logic, mathematics, astronomy—*schēma* was widely used in the sense of "outward shape," *figura* was always used for this purpose in Latin. Thus side by side with the original plastic signification and overshadowing it, there appeared a far more general concept of grammatical, rhetorical, logical, mathematical—and later even of musical and choreographic—form. To be sure, the original plastic sense was not entirely lost, for *typos,* "imprint," and *plasis, plasma,* "plastic form," were often rendered by *figura* as the radical *fig-* suggested. From the meaning of *typos* developed the use of *figura* as "imprint of the seal," a metaphor with a venerable history running from Aristotle (*De memoria et reminiscentia,* 450a, 31: *hē kinēsis ensēmainetai hoion typon tina tou aisthēmatos* ["the movement implies some impression of the thing sensed"], through Augustine (*Epist.,* 162, 4 [*Patrologia Latina,* XXXIII, col. 706], and Isidore (*Differentiae,* 1, 528 [*Patrologia Latina,* LXXXIII, col. 63]), to Dante (*come figura in cera si suggella* ["as a seal is stamped in wax"], *Purg.,* 10, 45, or *Par.,* 27, 52).[4] However, it was not only the plastic sense of *typos,* but also its inclination toward the universal, lawful, and exemplary (cf. the combination with *nomikōs,* Aristotle, *Politics,* II, 7, 1341b, 31) that exerted an influence on *figura,* and this in turn helped to efface the already faint dividing line with *forma.* The connection with words such as *plasis* increased the tendency of *figura*—which was probably present from the very beginning but developed only slowly—to expand in the direction of "statue," "image," "portrait," to impinge on the domain of *statua* and even of *imago, effigies, species, simulacrum.* Thus, though we may say in general that in Latin usage *figura* takes the place of *schēma,* this does not exhaust the force of the word, the *potestas verbi: figura* is broader, sometimes more plastic, in any case more dynamic and radiant than *schēma.* To be sure, *schēma* itself in Greek is more dynamic than the word as we use it; in Aristotle, for example, mimic gestures, especially of actors, are called *schēmata;* the meaning of dynamic form is by no means foreign to *schēma;* but *figura* developed this element of movement and transformation much further.[5]

Lucretius uses *figura* in the Greek philosophical sense, but in an extremely individual, free, and significant way. He starts with the general concept of "figure," which occurs in every possible shading from the plastic figure shaped by man (*manibus tractata figura,* 4, 230) to the purely geometric outline (2, 778; 4, 503); he transposes the term from the plastic and visual to the auditory sphere, when (in 4, 556) he speaks of the *figura verborum* ("the figure of words").[6] The important transition from the form to its imitation, from model to copy, may best be noted in the passage dealing with the resemblance of children to their parents, the mixture of seeds, and heredity; with children who are *utriusque figurae* ("of both *figurae*"), resembling both father and mother, and who often reflect *proavorum figuras* ("the *figurae* of their ancestors"), and so on: *inde Venus varias producit sorte figuras* ("thence Venus brought forth diverse *figurae* in turn") (4, 1223). Here we see that only *figura* could serve for this play on model and copy; *forma* and *imago* are too solidly anchored in one or the other of the two meanings; *figura* is more concrete and dynamic than *forma.* Here, of course, as in connection with later poets, we should not forget what a fine last foot for a hexameter is provided by *figura* in all its inflectional forms.[7] A special variant of the meaning "copy" occurs in Lucretius' doctrine of the structures that peel off things like membranes and float round in the air, his Democritean doctrine of the "film images" (Diels), or *eidola,* which he takes in a materialistic sense. These he calls *simulacra, imagines, effigies,* and sometimes *figurae;* and consequently it is in Lucretius that we first find the word employed in the sense of "dream image," "figment of fancy," "ghost."

These variants had great vitality, and were to enjoy a significant career; "model," "copy," "figment," "dream image"—all these meanings clung to *figura.* But it was in still another sphere that Lucretius developed his most ingenious use of the word. As we know, he professed the cosmogony of Democritus and Epicurus, according to which the world is built up of atoms. He calls the atoms *primordia, principia, corpuscula, elementa, semina,* and in a very general sense, he also called them *corpora, quorum concursus motus ordo positura figura*[8] (1, 685, and 2, 1021) ("bodies whose combination, motion, order, position, *figura"*) brings forth the things of the world. But though small, the atoms are material and formed: they have infinitely diverse shapes; and so it comes about that he often calls them "forms," *figurae,* and that conversely one may often translate *figurae,* as Diels has done, by "atoms." [9] The numerous atoms are in constant motion; they move about in the void, combine and repel one another: a dance of figures. This use of the word does not seem to have gone beyond Lucretius; the *Thesaurus* cites only one other example of it in Claudian (*Rufinum* 1, 17), at the end of the fourth century. In this small sphere, Lucretius' most original creation was without influence; but there is no doubt that of all the authors I have studied in connection with *figura,* it was Lucretius who made the most brilliant, though not the most historically important contribution.

In Cicero's frequent and extremely flexible use of the word, every variation of the concept of form that could possibly have been suggested by his political, publicistic, juridical, and philosophical activity, seems to be represented; and his use of the word reveals his lovable, volatile, and vacillating nature. Often he applies it to man, sometimes in tones of pathos. In *Pro S. Roscio* (63), he writes: *portentum atque monstrum certissimum est, esse aliquem humana specie et figura, qui tantum immanitate bestias vicerit, ut . . .* ("it is unquestionably an unnatural and monstrous thing, that a being in human form and *figura* should exist so far surpassing the wild beasts in savagery that . . ."). And in *Pro Q. Roscio* (20) *tacita corporis figura* ("the silent *figura* of a body") is the silent mien whose mere appearance betrays the scoundrel. The limbs and inner organs, animals, utensils, stars, in short all perceptible things have *figura*, and so do the gods and the universe as a whole. The sense of "appearance" and even "semblance" contained in the Greek *schēma* emerges clearly when he says that the tyrant has only *figura hominis* ("the semblance of a man") and that immaterial conceptions of God are without *figura* and *sensus* ("appearance and perception"). Clear distinctions between *figura* and *forma* are rare (e.g., *De natura deorum* I, 90; cf. note 7 above), and neither is confined to the realm of the visual; Cicero speaks of *figura vocis* ("of the voice"), *figura negotii* ("types of occupation"), and quite frequently of *figurae dicendi* ("figures of speech"). Of course geometric and stereometric forms also possess a *figura*. However, *figura* in the sense of copy or image is scarcely developed in Cicero. In *De natura deorum* (I, 71), to be sure, it is said that Cotta, one of the participants in the dialogue, might more readily understand the words *quasi corpus* ("a semblance of body") of the gods, *si in cereis fingeretur aut fictilibus figuris* ("if it were waxen images or clay figures"), and in *De divinatione* (1, 23) he speaks of the *figura* of a rock which is not unlike a little Pan. But this does not suffice, for the *figura* of which he is speaking is that of the clay or stone, not of what is represented.[10] Cicero uses the word *imagines* for the *schēmata* of Democritus and Lucretius, which emanate from the body (*a corporibus enim solidis et a certis figuris vult fluere imagines Democritus* ["Democritus would have it that phantoms emanate from solid bodies and from actual *figurae*"] *De divinatione,* 2, 137),[11] and in Cicero the images of the gods are usually called *signa,* never *figurae.* As an example we may cite the malicious joke against Verres (2, 2, 89): Verres planned to steal a precious statue of a god in a Sicilian city, but fell in love with his landlord's wife: *contemnere etiam signum illud Himerae jam videbatur quod eum multo magis figura et lineamenta hospitae delectabant* ("he seemed now even to despise that statue of Himera, so much more did the *figura* and features of his hostess delight him").[12] There is no sign of any such bold innovations as in Lucretius. Cicero's contribution consisted mainly in introducing the word in the sense of perceptible form to the educated language. He used it chiefly in his philosophical and rhetorical works, most frequently in his essay on the nature of the gods. In these works he tried to devise what today we should call an all-embracing concept of form. It is not only because of his well-known preoccupation with well-rounded oratorical periods that he seldom contents himself with *figura* alone, but usually piles up several related words with a view to expressing a whole: *formā et figura, conformatio quaedam et figura totius oris et corporis, habitus et figura,*

humana species et figura, vis et figura ("form and
figura," "a certain arrangement and *figura* of the
whole face and body," "appearance and *figura*," "the
human appearance and *figura*," "force and *figura*"),
and many more of the same kind. His striving for a
comprehensive view of the phenomenal world is un-
mistakable, and he may have communicated some of it
to the Roman reader. But he lacked the right kind of
talent and his eclectic attitude made it impossible for
him to work out and formulate a compelling idea of
form; his concept remained hazy. We must content
ourselves with the richness and balance of his words.
What is more important for the subsequent development of *figura* is something else: it is in Cicero and
the author of the *Ad Herennium* that it occurs for the
first time as a technical term in rhetoric, rendering
the *schēmata* or *charaktēres lexeōs,* the three levels of
style, which in *Ad Herennium* (4, 8, 11) are designated as *figura gravis, mediocris,* and *extenuata* ("the
grand, the middle, the simple *figura*"), and in *De
oratore* (3, 199, and 212) as *plena, mediocris,* and *te-
nuis* ("full, middle, plain"). However, Cicero (as Emil
Vetter, author of the article *"Figura"* in *Thesaurus
Linguae Latinae* expressly notes [VI, part 1, col. 731,
ll. 80 f.]) does not yet use the word as a technical term
for the ornamental circumlocutions that we call "figures of speech." Though he knows them and describes
them at length, he does not like later writers call them
figurae, but—again pleonastically—*formae et lumina
orationis* ("forms and ornaments of speech"). He does
employ the turn *figura dicendi,* or more frequently
forma et figura dicendi, not in a strict technical sense
but simply to denote a mode of eloquence, either in a
general sense when he wishes to say that there are innumerable kinds of eloquence (*De oratore,* 3, 34) or

individually when he says that Curio *suam quandam expressit quasi formam figuramque dicendi* ("has expressed as it were his own special pattern and figure of oratory," ibid., 2, 98). The students at the schools of rhetoric, where Cicero's treatises on eloquence soon became a canon, became accustomed to this combination.

Thus by the end of the republican era, *figura* was firmly ingrained in the language of philosophy and cultivated discourse, and during the first century of the Empire its possibilities continued to develop. As one may well imagine, it is the poets who were most interested in the shades of meaning between model and copy, in changing form and the deceptive likenesses that walk in dreams. Catullus (*Attis*, 62) has the characteristic passage: *Quod enim genus figurae est ego quod non obierim?* ("for what kind of *figura* is there that I had not?") Propertius[13] writes: (3, 24, 5) *mixtam te varia laudavi saepe figura* ("I often praised the blending of thy varied *figura*") or (4, 2, 21) *opportuna meast cunctis natura figuris* ("my nature finds every *figura* suitable"). And speaking, in the magnificent conclusion of his *Panegyricus ad Messalam,* of death's power to change the forms of man, he employs the words *mutata figura* ("changed *figura*"); and Virgil (*Aeneid,* 10, 641) in describing the phantom of Aeneas that appears to Turnus, writes *morte obita qualis fama est volitare figuras* ("*figurae* such as, they say, flit about after death"). But the richest source for *figura* in the sense of changing form is of course Ovid. To be sure, he uses *forma* freely in the same sense when the metre calls for a dissyllabic word; but most often he employs *figura*. He has an impressive store of combinations at his command: *figuram mutare, variare, vertere, retinere, inducere sumere, deponere, perdere.* The following little collection may give an idea of the countless ways in which he employs the word:

> . . . *tellus . . . partimque figuras / rettulit antiquas*
> (*Metamorphoses*, 1, 436);
> . . . *se mentitis superos celasse figuris* (ibid., 5, 326);
> *sunt quibus in plures ius est transire figuras* (ibid., 8, 730);
> . . . *artificem simulatoremque figurae / Morphea* (ibid., 11, 634);
> *ex aliis alias reparat natura figuras* (ibid., 15, 253);
> *animam . . . in varias doceo migrare figuras* (ibid., 15, 172);
> *lympha figuras / datque capitque novas* (ibid., 15, 308).

> (the earth . . . in part restored the ancient shapes; the gods hid themselves in lying shapes; there are some who have power to take on many shapes; Morpheus, the skillful artificer and imitator of [man's] shape; nature builds up forms from other forms; I teach that the soul . . . passes through various forms; water gives and receives new forms).

There is also a fine example of the imprint of the seal:

> *Utque novis facilis signatur cera figuris*
> *Nec manet ut fuerat nec formas servat easdem,*
> *Sed tamen ipsa eadem est . . .* (ibid., 15, 169 ff.).

> (And as the soft wax is stamped with new *figurae,* and does not remain as it was nor retain the same forms, though it remains itself the same . . .)

In addition, *figura* already appears quite plainly in Ovid as "copy," as for example, in *Fasti* (9, 278): *globus immensi parva figura poli* ("a globe, a small figure of the vast vault of heaven"), or in *Heroides* (14, 97) and *Ex Ponto* (2, 8, 64); in the sense of "letter"

which had already been given it by Varro, *ducere
consuescat multas manus una figuras* (*Ars amoris*, 3,
493) ("let one hand be accustomed to tracing many
figures"); finally, as "position" in love play: *Venerem
iungunt per mille figuras* ("They embrace in a thousand *figurae*") (*Ars*, 2, 679). Throughout Ovid *figura*
is mobile, changeable, multiform, and deceptive. The
word is also used skillfully by Manilius, author of the
Astronomica, who apart from the meanings already
mentioned, employs it (as well as *signum* and *forma*)
in the sense of "constellation." It occurs in the sense
of dream figment in Lucan and Statius.

In Vitruvius the architect we find something very
different both from these meanings and from those
that we shall find in the rhetoricians. In his writings
figura is architectural and plastic form, or in any case
the reproduction of such form, the architect's plan;
here there is no trace of deception or transformation;
in his language *figurata similitudine,* (7, 5, 1) does
not mean "by dissimulation," but "by creating a likeness." Often *figura* means "ground plan" (*modice
picta operis futuri figura,* slightly tinted, a plan of the
future work 1, 2, 2), and *universae figurae species* or
summa figuratio, signifies the general form of a build-
ing or a man (he often compares the two from the
standpoint of symmetry). Despite his occasional mathematical use of the word, *figura* (as well as *fingere*)
has a definitely plastic significance for him and for
other technical writers of the period; thus in Festus
(98), *crustulum cymbi figura*[14] ("a little cake shaped
like a boat") in Celsus, *venter reddit mollia, figurata*
(2, 5, 5) ("the belly gives forth soft, formed notions"),
in Columella, *ficos comprimunt in figuram stellarum
floscularumque* (12, 15, 5) ("they press figs into the
shape of stars and little flowers"). Even in this detail
Pliny the Elder, who belonged to a different social and

cultural class, is a far richer source; in his work every
shading of the concepts of form and species is represented. The transition from form to portrait is clearly
discernible in the memorable beginning of his thirty-
fifth book, in which he deplores the decline of portrait
painting: *Imaginum quidem pictura, qua maxime si-
miles in aevum propagantur figurae . . .* ("The painting of portraits, whereby extremely lifelike *figurae*
were transmitted down through the ages"); and somewhat later, when he speaks of the books illustrated
with portraits, a technique invented by Varro: *imaginum amorem flagrasse quondam testes sunt . . .
et Marcus Varro . . . insertis . . . septingentorum
illustrium . . . imaginibus: non passus intercidere
figuras, aut vetustatem aevi contra homines valere, inventor muneris etiam diis invidiosi, quando immor-
talitatem non solum dedit, verum etiam in omnes ter-
ras misit, ut praesentes esse ubique credi possent.*
("That there was a keen passion for portraits in olden
days . . . is shown by . . . Marcus Varro . . . who
inserted in his works portraits of 700 famous people:
not allowing their likenesses to disappear or the passing of time to prevail against men, and thus being the
inventor of a benefit which even the gods might envy,
for he not only bestowed immortality but also sent it
all over the world, that those concerned might be felt
to be present everywhere.")

The juridical literature of the first century has a
few passages in which *figura* means "empty outward
form" or "semblance." In *Digest*, 28, 5, 70, we find:
*non solum figuras sed vim quoque condicionis conti-
nere* (Proculus) and in *Digest*, 50, 16, 116: *Mihi La-
beo videtur verborum figuram sequi, Proculus mentem*
(Javolenus). ("It seems to me that Labes followed the
figura of the words, but Proculus their intention.")

But from the standpoint of its future destinies the

most important thing that happened to *figura* in the first century was the refinement of the concept of the rhetorical figure. The result has come down to us in the ninth book of Quintilian. The idea is older, it is Greek; and as we have seen above, it had already been expressed in Latin by Cicero; but Cicero did not yet use the word *figura,* and moreover the technique of the figure of speech seems to have been very much refined after his time in the course of endless discussions on rhetorical questions. When the word was first used in this sense cannot be exactly determined; probably soon after Cicero, as may be presumed from the title of a book (*De figuris sententiarum,* by Annaeus Cornutus) mentioned in Gellius (9, 10, 5), and from the remarks and allusions of both Senecas[15] and of Pliny the Younger. The development was only natural, since the Greek term was *schēma.* In general we must assume that the technical use of the word had developed earlier and more richly than can be demonstrated by the sources that have come down to us; that, for example, the figures of the syllogism (the *schēmata syllogismou* originated with Aristotle himself) must have been mentioned much earlier in Latin than in Boethius or the pseudo-Augustinian *Book of Categories.*

In the last section of the eighth book and in the ninth book of the *Institutio oratoria,* Quintilian gives a detailed account of the theory of tropes and figures. This disquisition, which seems to represent a comprehensive critique of former opinions and works, became the fundamental work on the subject, and all later efforts were based on it. Quintilian distinguishes tropes from figures; trope is the more restricted concept, referring to the use of words and phrases in a sense other than literal; figure, on the other hand, is a form of discourse which deviates from the normal and most obvious usage. The aim of a figure is not, as in all tropes, to substitute words for other words; figures can be formed from words used in their proper meaning and order. Basically all discourse is a forming, a figure, but the word is employed only for formations that are particularly developed in a poetic or rhetorical sense. Thus he distinguishes between simple (*carens figuris, aschēmatistos* ["lacking in figures"]) and figurative (*figuratus, eschēmatismenos*) modes of speech. The distinction between trope and figure proves to be difficult. Quintilian himself often hesitates before classifying a turn of speech as one or the other; in later usage *figura* is generally regarded as the higher concept, including trope, so that any unliteral or indirect form of expression is said to be as figurative. As tropes Quintilian names and describes metaphor, synecdoche (*mucronem pro gladio; puppim pro navi* ("blade for sword; prow for ship")), metonymy (Mars for war; Virgil for Virgil's works), antonomasia (Pelides for Achilles), and many more; he divides figures into those involving content and those involving words (*figurae sententiarum* and *verborum*). As *figurae sententiarum* he lists: the rhetorical question which the orator himself answers; the various ways of anticipating objections (prolepsis); the affectation of drawing judges or audience into one's confidence; prosopopoeia, in which one puts words into the mouths of other persons, such as one's adversary, or of personifications, such as the fatherland; the solemn apostrophe; the embroidering of a narrative with concrete detail, *evidentia* or *illustratio;* the various forms of irony; aposiopesis or *obticentia* or *interruptio,* in which one "swallows" part of the phrase; affected repentance over something one has said; and so on; but the figure which was then regarded as the most important and seemed before all others to merit the name of figure was the hidden allusion in its diverse forms. Roman orators had developed a refined technique of expressing or insinuating something without saying it, in most cases of course something which for political or tactical reasons, or simply for the sake of effect, had best remain secret or at least unspoken. Quintilian speaks of the importance attached to training in this technique in the schools of rhetoric, and tells us how speakers would invent special cases, *controversiae figuratae,* in order to perfect and distinguish themselves in it. As "word figures" he finally mentions intentional solecisms, rhetorical repetitions, antitheses, phonetic resemblances, omissions of a word, asyndeton, climax, etc.

His exposition of tropes and figures, of which we have given only the barest essentials, is accompanied by an abundance of examples and detailed studies of the different forms and the distinctions between them; it takes up a large part of his eighth and ninth books. The system that he set forth was a very elaborate one; yet it seems likely that for a rhetorician Quintilian was relatively free in his thinking and as disinclined to excessive hairsplitting as the spirit of the times permitted. The art of the hinting, insinuating, obscuring circumlocution, calculated to ornament a statement or to make it more forceful or mordant, had achieved a versatility and perfection that strike us as strange if not absurd. These turns of speech were called *figurae.* The Middle Ages and the Renaissance, as we know, still attached a good deal of importance to the science of figures of speech. For the theorists of style of the twelfth and thirteenth century the *Ad Herennium*[16] was the main source of wisdom.

So much for the history of the word *figura* in pagan antiquity; a few grammatical, rhetorical, and logical extensions follow automatically from the meanings already stated, and some have been mentioned by other writers.[17, 18] But the meaning which the Church Fathers gave the word on the basis of the development described in the previous pages was of the greatest historical importance.

II. Figura *in the Phenomenal Prophecy of the Church Fathers*

The strangely new meaning of *figura* in the Christian world is first to be found in Tertullian, who uses it very frequently. In order to clarify its meaning we shall discuss a few passages. In his polemic *Adversus Marcionem* (3, 16) Tertullian speaks of Oshea, son of Nun, whom Moses (according to Num. 13:16) named Jehoshua (Joshua):

> ... *et incipit vocari Jesus.* ... *Hanc prius dicimus figuram futurorum fuisse. Nam quia Jesus Christus secundum populum, quod sumus nos, nati in saeculi desertis, introducturus erat in terram promissionis, melle et lacte manantem, id est vitae aeternae possessionem, qua nihil dulcius; idque non per Moysen, id est, non per legis disciplinam, sed per Jesum, id est per evangelii gratiam provenire habebat* (Vulgar Latin form for "was to happen"), *circumcisis nobis petrina acie, id est Christi praeceptis; Petra enim Christus; ideo is vir, qui in huius sacramenti imagines parabatur, etiam nominis dominici inauguratus est figura, Jesus cognominatus.*

For the first time he is called Jesus. ... This, then, we first observe, was a figure of things to come. For inasmuch as Jesus Christ was to introduce a new people, that is to say us, who are born in the wilderness of this world, into the promised land flowing with milk and honey, that is to say, into the possession of eternal life, than which nothing is sweeter; and that,

too, was not to come about through Moses, that is to
say, through the discipline of the Law, but through
Jesus, that is, through the grace of the gospel, our
circumcision being performed by a knife of stone, that
is to say, by Christ's precepts—for Christ is a rock;
therefore that great man, who was prepared as a type
of this sacrament, was even consecrated in figure with
the Lord's name, and was called Jesus.)

Here the naming of Joshua-Jesus is treated as a
prophetic event foreshadowing things to come.[19] Just as
Joshua and not Moses led the people of Israel into
the promised land of Palestine, so the grace of Jesus,
and not the Jewish law, leads the "second people" into
the promised land of eternal beatitude. The man who
appeared as the prophetic annunciation of this still
hidden mystery, *qui in huius sacramenti imagines pa-
rabatur,* was introduced under the *figura* of the divine
name. Thus the naming of Joshua-Jesus is a phenomenal prophecy or prefiguration of the future Saviour;
figura is something real and historical which an-
nounces something else that is also real and historical.
The relation between the two events is revealed by an
accord or similarity. Thus, for example, Tertullian
says in *Adversus Marcionem* (5, 7): *Quare Pascha
Christus, si non Pascha figura Christi per similitudi-
nem sanguinis salutaris et pecoris Christi?* ("How is
Christ the Passover, except inasmuch as the Passover
is a figure of Christ through the likeness of the saving
blood and of the flock of Christ?") Often vague simi-
larities in the structure of events or in their attendant
circumstances suffice to make the *figura* recognizable;
to find it, one had to be determined to interpret in a
certain way. As for example, when (ibid., 3, 17, or
Adv. Iudaeos, 14) the two sacrificial goats of Lev. 16:
7 ff. are interpreted as figures of the first and second

coming of Christ; or when, as in *De anima,* 43 (cf. also *De Monogamia,* 5) Eve, as *figura Ecclesiae,* is developed from Adam as *figura Christi: Si enim Adam de Christo figuram dabat, somnus Adae mors erat Christi dormituri in mortem, ut de iniuria* (wound) *perinde lateris eius vera mater viventium figuraretur ecclesia.*[20] ("For if Adam provided a *figura* of Christ, the sleep of Adam was the death of Christ who was to sleep in death, that precisely by the wound in his side should be figured the Church, the mother of all living.")

We shall speak later on of how the desire to interpret in this way arose. At all events the aim of this sort of interpretation was to show that the persons and events of the Old Testament were prefigurations of the New Testament and its history of salvation. Here it should be noted that Tertullian expressly denied that the literal and historical validity of the Old Testament was diminished by the figural interpretation. He was definitely hostile to spiritualism and refused to consider the Old Testament as mere allegory; according to him, it had real, literal meaning throughout, and even where there was figural prophecy, the figure had just as much historical reality as what it prophesied. The prophetic figure, he believed, is a concrete historical fact, and it is fulfilled by concrete historical facts. For this Tertullian uses the term *figuram implere* (*Adversus Marcionem,* 4, 40: *figuram sanguinis sui salutaris implere* ["to fulfill the figure of his saving blood"]) or *confirmare* (*De fuga in persecutione,* XI: *Christo confirmante figuras suas* ["Christ confirming his figures"]). From now on we shall refer to the two events as figure and fulfillment.

Tertullian was a staunch realist, as we know in other connections. For him the *figura,* in the simple sense of "form," is a part of the substance, and in *Ad-*

versus Marcionem (5, 20) he equates it with the flesh. Just above (4, 40), he had spoken of bread in the Eucharist:

> *Corpus illum suum fecit "Hoc est corpus meum" dicendo, "id est, figura corporis mei." Figura autem non fuisset, nisi veritatis esset corpus. Ceterum vacua res, quod est phantasma, figuram capere non posset. Aut si propterea panem corpus sibi finxit, quia corporis carebat veritate, ergo panem debuit tradere pro nobis. Faciebat ad vanitatem Marcionis, ut panis crucifigeretur. Cur autem panem corpus suum appellat, et non magis peponem, quem Marcion cordis loco habuit? Non intelligens veterem fuisse istam figuram corporis Christi, dicentis per Ieremiam* [11:19]: *Adversus me cogitaverunt cogitatum dicentes, Venite, coniiciamus lignum in panem eius, scilicet crucem in corpus eius.*

> (He made it his own body, saying, "This is my body, that is, the figure of my body." For there could not have been a figure unless there were a true body. An empty thing, that is, a phantom, could not take on a figure. If, therefore, he pretended the bread to be his body, because he lacked the reality of a body, then he must have given bread for us. It would suit Marcion's fantastic claim that the bread should be crucified. But why does he call his body bread and not rather a melon, such as Marcion must have had in place of a heart? He did not understand how ancient was that figure of the body of Christ, who said through Jer. (11:19): They have devised devices against me, saying, Come, let us put wood upon his bread, which means, of course, the cross upon his body.)

These powerful sentences—in the following the wine, *figura sanguinis* ("figure of the blood") is represented no less forcefully as *probatio carnis* ("a proof of the flesh")[21]—show clearly how concretely both terms were intended in Tertullian's figural interpretation; in every case the only spiritual factor is the understanding, *intellectus spiritualis,* which recognizes the figure in the fulfillment. The Prophets, he says in *De resurrectione carnis* (19 ff.), did not speak only in images; for if they had, we should be unable to recognize the images; a great deal should be taken quite literally, as also in the New Testament: *nec omnia umbrae, sed et corpora; ut in ipsum quoque Dominum insigniora quaeque luce clarius praedicantur; nam et virgo concepit in utero, non figurate; et peperit Emanuelem nobiscum Jesum Christum, non oblique.* ("And not all are shadows, but there are bodies also; so that we have prophecies even about the Lord himself, which are clearer than the day. For it was not figuratively that the Virgin conceived in her womb; and not by a metaphor that she gave birth to Emmanuel, God with us, Christ Jesus.") And he resolutely attacks those who twist the clearly proclaimed resurrection of the dead into an "imaginary meaning" (*in imaginariam significationem distorquent*). There are many passages of this kind, in which he combats the spiritualizing tendencies of contemporary groups. His realism stands out still more clearly in the relation between figure and fulfillment, for sometimes the one and sometimes the other seems to possess a higher degree of historical concreteness. In *Adversus Marcionem* (4, 40), for example (*an ipse erat, qui . . . tamquam ovis coram tendente sic os non aperturus, figuram sanguinis sui salutaris implere concupiscebat?* ["was it not that he, who . . . as a sheep before her shearers, was not to open his mouth, desired so ardently to fulfill the figure of his saving blood?"]), the figure of the servant of God as a lamb seems to be a mere simile; in another passage the Law as a whole is juxtaposed to Christ as its fulfillment (ibid., 5, 19: *de umbra transfertur ad corpus, id est, de figuris ad veritatem* ["It is transferred from the shadow to the substance, that is, from figures to the reality"]). It might seem that in the first case the simile and in the second case the abstraction give the figure a lesser force of reality. But there is no lack of examples in which the figure has the greater concreteness. In *De baptismo* (5), where the pool of Bethesda appears as a figure of the baptism, we find the sentence: *figura ista medicinae corporalis spiritalem medicinam canebat, ea forma qua semper carnalia in figuram spiritalium antecedunt.* ("This figure of bodily healing told of a spiritual healing, according to the rule by which carnal things come first as a figure of spiritual things.") But the one and the other, the pool of Bethesda and the baptism, are concretely real, and all that is spiritual about them is the interpretation or effect; for the baptism too, as Tertullian himself hastens to add (ibid., 7), is a carnal action: *sic et in nobis carnaliter currit unctio, sed spiritaliter proficit; quomodo et ipsius baptismi carnalis actus, quod in aqua mergimur, spiritalis effectus, quod delictis liberamur.* ("Thus with us also the unction runs down carnally, but its profit is spiritual; in the same way as the act of baptism is carnal, in that we are plunged in water, but its effects are spiritual, namely that we are freed from transgression.") These examples give us the feeling that even in the first two cases Tertullian had in mind not only a metaphorical but also a real lamb, and not only the law in the abstract but also the era of the law as a historical era.

And sometimes two statements are related to one another as figure and fulfillment, as in *De fuga in persecutione,* 11: *certe quidem bonus pastor animam pro pecoribus ponit; ut Moyses, non Domino adhuc Christo revelato, etiam in se figurato, ait: Si perdis*

hunc populum, inquit, et me pariter cum eo disperde
[Exod. 32:32]. *Ceterum, Christo confirmante figuras
suas, malus pastor est . . .* [John 10:12]. ("Assuredly
a good shepherd lays down his life for his sheep, even
as Moses said, when the Lord Christ had not yet been
revealed, but was shadowed forth in himself: If you
destroy this people, said he, destroy me also along with
them [Exod. 32:32]. And Christ himself, confirming
these figures, says: But the evil shepherd, etc. [John
10:12].") But both statements are historical events,
and moreover it is not so much the statements as
Moses and Christ themselves who are related as figure
and fulfillment.[22] The fulfillment is often designated
as *veritas,* as in an example above, and the figure cor-
respondingly as *umbra* or *imago;* but both shadow
and truth are abstract only in reference to the meaning first concealed, then revealed; they are concrete
in reference to the things or persons which appear as
vehicles of the meaning. Moses is no less historical and
real because he is an *umbra* or *figura* of Christ, and
Christ, the fulfillment, is no abstract idea, but also a
historical reality. Real historical figures are to be interpreted spiritually (*spiritaliter interpretari*), but the
interpretation points to a carnal, hence historical fulfillment (*carnaliter adimpleri: De resurrectione,* 20)—
for the truth has become history or flesh.

From the fourth century on, the usage of the word
figura and the method of interpretation connected
with it are fully developed in nearly all the Latin
Church writers.[23] Sometimes to be sure—a practice
that later became general—common allegory was also
termed *figura;* in *Divinae institutiones* (2, 10) Lactantius interprets south and north as *figurae vitae et mor-
tis* ("figures of life and death"), day and night as true
and false faith; yet the Christian notion of prefiguration and fulfillment immediately enters in: *etiam in*

hoc praescius futurorum Deus fecit, ut ex iis, et verae religionis, et falsarum superstitionum imago quaedam ostenderetur ("and here also, in his foreknowledge of the future, God caused that an image, as it were, should be displayed in these things both of true religion and of false superstitions"). And thus *figura* often appears in the sense of "deeper meaning in reference to future things": the sufferings of Jesus *non fuerunt inania, sed habuerunt figuram et significationem* ("were not vain but had figure and significance") and he speaks in this connection of divine works in general *quorum vis et potentia valebat quidem in praesens, sed declarabat aliquid in futurum* ("whose force and power were of avail indeed in the present time, but also foreshowed something in the future"). This conception also dominates his eschatology which, following a speculation then widespread, interpreted the six days of Creation as six millennia, which were then almost at an end; the millennial kingdom was imminent (ibid., 7, 14): *saepe diximus, minora et exigua magnorum figuras et praemonstrationes esse; ut hunc diem nostrum qui ortu solis occasuque finitur, diei magni speciem gerere, quem circuitus annorum mille determinat. Eodem modo figuratio terreni hominis caelestis populi praeferebat in posterum fictionem.*[24] ("We have frequently said that small and trivial things are figures and foreshadowings of great things; thus, this day of ours, which is bounded by sunrise and sunset, bears the likeness of that great day which is circumscribed by the passing of a thousand years. In the same way the *figuratio* of man on earth carried with it a parable of the heavenly people yet to be.")

In most authors of the same period the figural interpretation and its most familiar examples are current coin,[25] as are the opposition between *figura* and *veritas.* But sometimes we encounter a more spiritual-ist, allegorical, and ethical mode of interpretation—as in Origen's Bible commentaries. In one passage, dealing with the sacrifice of Isaac—in other respects this is one of the most famous examples of the realistic type of figural interpretation—Rufinus, the Latin translator of Origen (*Patrologia Graeca,* 12, 209; the Greek original has been lost) has the following: *Sicut in Domino corporeum nihil est, etiam tu in his omni-bus corporeum nihil sentias: sed in spiritu generes etiam tu filium Isaac, cum habere coeperis fructum spiritus, gaudium, pacem.* ("As there is no bodily ele-ment in the Lord, so do you also see nothing corporal in all these things; but you also may bear your son Isaac in the spirit, when you begin to possess the fruit of the spirit, joy, and peace.") Origen, to be sure, is far from being as abstractly allegorical as, for exam-ple, Philo; in his writings, the events of the Old Testa-ment seem alive, with a direct bearing on the reader and his real life; yet in his fine explanation of the three-day journey in Exodus, for example (loc. cit., pp. 313 ff.), mystical and moral considerations seem def-initely to overshadow the strictly historical element.[26] The difference between Tertullian's more historical and realistic interpretation and Origen's ethical, alle-gorical approach reflects a current conflict, known to us from other early Christian sources: one party strove to transform the events of the New and still more of the Old Testament into purely spiritual happenings, to "spirit away" their historical character—the other wished to preserve the full historicity of the Scriptures along with the deeper meaning. In the West the latter tendency was victorious, although the spiritualists al-ways maintained a certain influence, as may be seen from the progress of the doctrine of the different meanings of Scripture; for while the adherents of this doctrine recognize the literal or historical sense, they sever its connection with the equally real prefiguration by setting up other, purely abstract interpretations beside or in place of the prefigural interpretation. St. Augustine played a leading part in the compromise between the two doctrines. On the whole he favored a living, figural interpretation, for his thinking was far too concrete and historical to content itself with pure abstract allegory.

The whole classical tradition was very much alive in St. Augustine, and of this his use of the word *figura* is one more indication. In his writings we find it expressing the general notion of form in all its traditional variants, static and dynamic, outline and body; it is applied to the world, to nature as a whole, and to the particular object; along with *forma, color,* and so on, it stands for the outward appearance (*Epist.,* 120, 10, or 146, 3); or it may signify the variable aspect over against the imperishable essence. It is in this last sense that he interprets I Cor. 7:31: *Peracto quippe iudicio tunc esse desinet hoc coelum et haec terra, quando incipiet esse coelum novum et terra nova. Mutatione namque rerum non omni modo interitu transibit hic mundus. Unde et apostolus dicit: praeterit enim figura huius mundi, volo vos sine sollicitudine esse. Figura enim praeterit, non natura (De civitate Dei,* 20, 14). ("When the judgment shall be finished, then this heaven and this earth shall cease to be, and a new heaven and a new earth shall begin. But this world will not be utterly consumed; it will only undergo a change; and therefore the Apostle says: The fashion [*figura*] of this world passeth away, and I would have you to be without care. The fashion [*figura*] goes away, not the nature.") [Trans. John Healey, Everyman edition. London, 1950, Vol. II, p. 289.] *Figura* appears also as idol, as dream figure or vision, as mathematical form; scarcely one of the many known variants is missing. But by far the most often it appears in the sense of prefiguration. Augustine explicitly adopted the figural interpretation of the Old Testament and emphatically recommended its use in sermons and missions (e.g., *De catechizandis rudibus,* III, 6), and developed on the method. Its whole repertory of interpretations passes us by in his work: Noah's ark is *praefiguratio ecclesiae* ("a prefiguration of the Church,") (*De civitate Dei* 15, 27); in several different ways Moses is *figura Christi* (e.g., *De civitate Dei,* 10, 8, or 18, 11); Aaron's *sacerdotium* is *umbra et figura aeterni sacerdotii* ("shadow and figure of the eternal priesthood") (ibid., 17, 6); Hagar, the slave woman, is a *figura* of the Old Testament, of the *terrena Jerusalem* ("earthly Jerusalem"), and Sarah of the New Testament, of the *superna Jerusalem civitas Dei* ("the heavenly Jerusalem, the city of God") (ibid., 16, 31; 17, 3; *Expos. ad Galatas,* 40); Jacob and Esau *figuram praebuerunt duorum populorum in Christianis et Iudeis* ("prefigured the two peoples of Jews and Christians") (*De civitate Dei,* 16, 42); the king of Judaea (*Christi*) *figuram prophetica unctione gestabant* (ibid., 17, 4) ("by being anointed by the prophets bore a prefiguration of the Christ."). These are only a few examples; the whole Old Testament, or at least its important figures and events, are all interpreted figurally; even where hidden meanings are found, as for example in Hannah's prayer of thanksgiving (I Sam. 2:1-10) in *De civ.,* 17, 4, the interpretation is not only allegorical but figural as well; Hannah's song of praise over the birth of her son Samuel is explained as a figure for the transformation of the old earthly kingdom and priesthood into the new heavenly kingdom and priesthood; she herself becomes a *figura ecclesiae.*

Augustine emphatically rejected the purely allegorical interpretation of the Holy Scriptures and dismissed the notion that the Old Testament was a kind of hermetic book that became intelligible only if one discarded the literal historical meaning and the vulgar interpretation. He held that every believer could gradually penetrate its sublime content. In *De trinitate* (11, 2) he writes: . . . *sancta scriptura parvulis congruens nullius generis rerum verba vitavit, ex quibus quasi gradatim ad divina atque sublimia noster intellectus velut nutritus assurgeret* ("the Holy Scriptures, as is fitting for little ones, did not shun any kind of verbal expression through which our understanding might be nourished and rise step by step to divine and sublime things"). And again, referring more plainly to the problem of figures: *Ante omnia, fratres, hoc in nomine Domini et admonemus, et praecipimus, ut quando auditis exponi sacramentum scripturae narrantis quae gesta sunt, prius illud quod lectum est credatis sic gestum, quomodo lectum est; ne substrato fundamento rei gestae, quasi in aere quaeratis aedificare* (*Serm.*, 2, 6)[27] ("Before all things, brethren, we admonish and command you in the name of the Lord, that when you hear an exposition of the mystery of the Scriptures telling of things that took place, you believe what is read to have actually taken place as the reading narrates; lest, undermining the foundation of actuality, you seek as it were to build in the air"). He took the view—which had long ago become part of the tradition—that the Old Testament was pure phenomenal prophecy, and he laid more stress than others on certain passages in the Pauline epistles of which we shall have more to say later on. The observances of the law *quas tamquam umbras futuri saeculi nunc respuunt Christiani, id tenentes, quod per illas umbras figurate promittebatur* ("which Christians now cast aside as mere shadows of the age to come, possessing as they do that which was promised in a figure by those shadows") and the sacraments *quae habuerunt promissivas figuras* ("which served as figures of promise"), are the letter of Scripture, precisely in the sense that their undoubted carnal and historical reality has, no less historically, been revealed and spiritually interpreted by the Christian fulfillment—and as we shall soon see, replaced by a new, more complete, and clearer promise. Consequently a Christian should hold *non ad legem operum, ex qua nemo iustificatur, sed ad legem fidei, ex qua iustus vivit (De spiritu et littera,* XIV, 23) ("not the works of the law, by which no man is justified, but to the law of faith, by which the just man lives"). The Jews of the Old Testament, *quando adhuc sacrificium verum, quod fideles norunt, in figuris praenuntiabatur, celebrabant figuram futurae rei; multi scientes, sed plures ignorantes (Enarr. in Psalm.,* 39, 12) ("when they still foretold in figures that true sacrifice which the faithful know, were celebrating figures of a reality to come in the future; for they knew many things, but were ignorant of even more"); while the latter-day Jews, and here he strikes a theme which was to run through all subsequent polemics against the Jews,[28] refused in their obdurate blindness to recognize this: *Non enim frustra Dominus ait Judaeis: si crederetis Moysi, crederetis et mihi; de me enim ille scripsit (Joan.,* 5, 46); *carnaliter quippe accipiendo legem, et eius promissa terrena rerum coelestium figuras esse nescientes (De civ.,* 20, 28) ("For the Lord spoke not idly . . . when He told the Jews, saying: 'Had ye believed Moses, you would have believed Me, for he wrote of Me.' For these men accepted the law in a carnal sense and did not understand its earthly promises as types [*figuras*] of heavenly

things.") But the "heavenly" fulfillment is not complete, and consequently, as in certain earlier writers
but more definitely in Augustine, the confrontation
of the two poles, figure and fulfillment, is sometimes
replaced by a development in three stages: the Law or
history of the Jews as a prophetic *figura* for the appearance of Christ; the incarnation as fulfillment of
this *figura* and at the same time as a new promise of
the end of the world and the Last Judgment; and
finally, the future occurrence of these events as ultimate fulfillment. In *Serm.*, 4, 8, we read: *Vetus enim
Testamentum est promissio figurata, novum Testamentum est promissio spiritualiter intellecta* ("The
Old Testament is a promise in figure, the New is a
promise understood after the spirit"), and still more
clearly in *Contra Faustinum*, 4, 2: *Temporalium quidem rerum promissiones Testamento Veteri contineri,
et ideo Vetus Testamentum appellari nemo nostrum
ambigit; et quod aeternae vitae promissio regnumque
coelorum ad Novum pertinet Testamentum: sed in
illis temporalibus figuras fuisse futurorum quae im-
plerentur in nobis, in quos finis saeculorum obvenit,
non suspicio mea, sed apostolicus intellectus est, di-
cente Paulo, cum de talibus loqueretur: Haec omnia
. . .* ("For we are all aware that the Old Testament
contains promises of temporal things, and that is why
it is called the Old Testament; and that the promise
of eternal life and the kingdom of heaven belongs to
the New Testament: but that in these temporal figures
there was the promise of future things, which were to
be fulfilled in us, on whom the ends of the world are
come, is no fantasy of mine, but the interpretation of
the apostles, as Paul says, speaking of these matters:
For all these things. . . .") And at this point Augustine quotes I Cor. 10:6 and 11. Although here the
ultimate fulfillment is regarded as imminent, it is

clear that Augustine has in mind two promises, one concealed and seemingly temporal in the Old Testament, the other clearly expressed and supratemporal in the Gospel. This gives the doctrine of the fourfold meaning of Scripture a far more realistic, historical, and concrete character, for three of the four meanings become concrete, historical, and interrelated, while only one remains purely ethical and allegorical—as Augustine explains in *De genesi ad litteram*, 1, 1: *In libris autem omnibus sanctis intueri oportet, quae ibi aeterna intimentur* ("In all the holy books those things are to be looked for which are indicated as having to do with eternity")—end of the world and eternal life, analogical interpretation; *quae futura praenuntientur* ("which foretell future events")—figural meaning in the strict sense, in the Old Testament the prefigurations of the coming of Christ; *quae agenda praecipiantur vel moneantur* ("which command or advise what we are to do")—ethical meaning.

Even though Augustine rejects abstract allegorical spiritualism and develops his whole interpretation of the Old Testament from the concrete historical reality, he nevertheless has an idealism which removes the concrete event, completely preserved as it is, from time and transposes it into a perspective of eternity. Such ideas were implicit in the notion of the incarnation of the Word; the figural interpretation of history paved the way for them, and they made their appearance at an early day. When Tertullian, for example, says (*Adversus Marcionem*, 3, 5) that in Isa. 50:6 *dorsum meum posui in flagella* (Vulgate, *corpus meum dedi percutientibus*) ("I gave my back to the smiters"), the future is represented figurally by past events, he adds that for God there is no *differentia temporis* ("difference of time"). But none among Augustine's precursors or contemporaries seems to have developed this idea so profoundly and completely as Augustine himself. Time and again he stresses the opposition which Tertullian felt only because of the perfect tense employed in the narrative; for example, in *De civ.*, 17, 8: *Scriptura sancta etiam de rebus gestis prophetans quodammodo in eo figuram delineat futurorum* ("the Holy Scripture, even when prophesying of things that are already done, outlines in a certain manner a figure of future things"); or in reference to a discrepancy between Psalm 113, *In exitu,* and the corresponding narrative in Exodus (*Enarr. in Psalm.*, 113, 1): *ne arbitremini nobis narrari praeterita, sed potius futura praedici . . . ut id, quod in fine saeculorum manifestandum reservabatur, figuris rerum atque verborum praecurrentibus nuntiaretur* ("Do not look upon as telling of the past, but rather as foretelling the future . . . that what was reserved to be made manifest at the end of the ages should be announced in material and verbal figures to those who came before"). Perhaps Augustine's view of the eternal character of the figures is best appreciated in a passage that does not refer expressly to figural interpretation: *Quid enim est praescientia, nisi scientia futurorum? Quid actem futurum est Deo qui omnia supergreditur tempora? Si enim scientia Dei res ipsas habet, non sunt ei futurae, sed praesentes; ac per hoc non jam praescientia, sed tantum scientia dici potest* (*De div. quaest. ad Simplicianum,* II, *qu.* 2, n. 2) ("For what is foreknowledge but knowledge of the future? But what is future to God who transcends all time? If God's knowledge contains these things, they are not future to Him but present; therefore it can be termed not foreknowledge, but simply knowledge").

The figural interpretation was of great practical use for the mission of the fourth and following centuries; it was constantly employed in sermons and religious

instruction, often, to be sure, mixed with purely allegorical and ethical interpretations. The *Formulae spi-*
ritalis intelligentiae[29] of Bishop Eucherius of Lyons
(early fifth century), educated at Lerins, is a textbook
of figural and ethical interpretation; from the sixth
century we have the *Instituta regularia divinae legis*
of Junilius, *Quaestor sacri palatii* (*Patrologia Latina*,
Vol. 68, cols. 15 ff.), which is a translation of a Greek
work influenced by the Antioch school; in its first
chapter we find the following doctrine: *Veteris Tes-*
tamenti intentio est Novum figuris praenuntiationi-
busque monstrare; Novi autem ad aeternae beatitu-
dinis gloriam humanas mentes accendere ("The
intention of the Old Testament is to point to the
New by figures and prophecies; that of the New is
to kindle the minds of men to the glory of eternal
beatitude"). A practical example of how the figural
interpretation was used in the instruction of new converts is provided by the explanation of the paschal
sacrifice in the second Sermon of Bishop Gaudentius
of Brescia (*Patrologia Latina*, 20, col. 855), who gives
us a perhaps unconscious expression of figural perspective when he says that the *figura* (preceding in time)
is not *veritas*, but *imitatio veritatis*. We find a good
many strange and farfetched figural interpretations,
often mixed with purely abstract, ethical allegory. But
the basic view that the Old Testament, both as a
whole and in its most important details, is a concrete
historical prefiguration of the Gospel, became a firmly
rooted tradition.

Now let us return to our semantic investigation and
ask how the Church Fathers arrived at the new sense
of *figura*. The earliest works of Christian literature
were written in Greek, and the word most often used
in them for "prefiguration"—in the *Epistle of Barna-*
bas for example—is *typos*. This leads to the presump-

tion—which may have come to the reader in connection with some of our quotations, the passages from Lactantius, for example—that *figura* passed directly from its general meaning of "formation" or "form" to its new signification; and indeed the usage of the oldest ecclesiastical writers makes this seem likely. When they write that persons or events of the Old Testament *figuram Christi (ecclesiae, baptismi, etc.) gerunt* or *gestant* ("provide a *figura* of Christ, the Church, baptism, etc."), that the Jewish people in all things *figuram nostram portat* ("bears our *figura*"), that the Holy Scripture *figuram delineat futurorum* ("delineates the *figura* of things to come"), *figura* in these sentences can simply be translated as "form." But then the idea of the *schēma* as molded by pre-Christian poetry and oratory—the rhetorical image or circumlocution that conceals, transforms, and even deceives— enters in. The opposition between *figura* and *veritas,* the interpretation *(exponere)* and unveiling *(aperire, revelare)*[30] of figures, the equation of *figura* with *umbra,* of *sub figura* with *sub umbra* (e.g., *ciborum,* ["of foodstuffs"], or in a more general sense, *legis* ["of the law"], the notion of a *figura* under which something other, future, true, lies concealed)—all this shows that the old sense of rhetorical image had survived, though it had moved from the purely nominalistic world of the schools of oratory and of Ovid's half playful myths into a realm both real and spiritual, hence authentic, significant, and existential. The distinction between figures of word and figures of substance that we find in Quintilian is resumed in the distinction between *figura verborum* and *figurae rerum,* word and prophetic events or phenomenal prophecies.

On this new basis the word has vastly extended its range of signification. We find *figura* as "deeper meaning," as for example in Sedulius (*ista res habet egre-giam figuram, Carm. pasch.,* 5, 384 f. ["this event has an extraordinary *figura*"]) and in Lactantius; as "de-ception" or "deceptive form" (Filastrius 61, *Liber de Haeresibus, Patrologia Latina,* Vol. 12, col. 1176) (*sub figura confessionis christianae*) ["under the *figura* of the Christian faith"] meaning "alleging to be Chris-tians"), or Sulpicius Severus, *De vita beati Martini,* 21, 1 (*Pastrologia Latina,* Vol. 20, col. 172), who says that the Devil *sive* [*se*] *in diversas figuras spiritalis nequi-tiae transtulisset* ("transformed himself into various *figurae* of spiritual wickedness"), or Leo the Great, *Epist.,* 98, 3 (*Patrologia Latina,* 54, 955): *lupum pasto-rali pelle nudantes, qua prius quoque figura tantum-modo convincebatur obtectus* ("stripping the wolf of his sheep's clothing, wherewith formerly in a figure he was shown to be concealed"); as an "empty" or "deceptive manner of speaking" or "evasion" (*per tot figuras ludimur,* Prudentius, *Peristephanon,* 2, 315 ["we are made sport of by all these *figurae*"]), or Ru-finus, *Apologia adversus Hieronymus,* 2, 22: *qualibus* (*Ambrosium*) *figuris laceret* ("figures with which he mangled Ambrose"); or simply as "discourse" or "word" (*te . . . incauta violare figura* ["I feared to hurt thee with an incautious figure"] Paulinus of Nola, *Carmina,* 11, 12); and finally in variations of the new meaning which scarcely permit of an appropriate translation: in the poetic *De actibus apostolorum* of the sixth-century subdeacon Arator (*Patrologia La-tina,* 68, cols. 83 ff.) we find the verses: *tamen illa figura, qua sine nulla vetus* (i.e., *Veteris Testamenti*) *subsistit littera, demun hac melius novitate manet* (Bk. 2, el. 361-3) ("but that figure, without which not a letter of the Old Testament exists, now at length endures to better purpose in the New"); and from just about the same time, a passage in the writings of

Bishop Avitus of Vienne (*Poema,* 5, 1. 284, *MG Auct. ant.,* VI, 2)[31] in which he speaks of the Last Judgment; just as God in killing the first-born in Egypt spared the houses daubed with blood, so may He recognize and spare the faithful by the sign of the Eucharist: *Tu cognosce tuam salvanda in plebe figuram* ("recognize thine own figure in the people that are to be saved").

Beside the opposition between *figura* and fulfillment or truth, there appears another, between *figura* and *historia; historia* or *littera* is the literal sense or the event related; *figura* is the same literal meaning or event in reference to the fulfillment cloaked in it, and this fulfillment itself is *veritas,* so that *figura* becomes a middle term between *littera-historia* and *veritas.* In this connection *figura* is roughly equivalent to *spiritus* or *intellectus spiritalis,* sometimes replaced by *figuralitas,* as in the following passage from the *Continentia Vergiliana* of Fulgentius (90, 1): *sub figuralitate historiae plenum hominis monstravimus statum* ("we have shown the whole state of mankind under the figure of history"). Of course *figura* and *historia* may often be used interchangeably (*ab historia in mysterium surgere* ["to rise from *historia* to mystery"]), says Gregory the Great (*Ezech.,* 1, 6, 3) and further on both *historiare* and *figurare* mean "to represent in images," "to illustrate," the first however only in the literal sense, the second also in the sense of "to interpret allegorically." [32]

Figura is not the only Latin word used for historic prefiguration; often we find the Greek terms *allegoria* and still more frequently *typus; allegoria* generally refers to any deeper meaning and not only to phenomenal prophecy, but the boundary is fluid, for *figura* and *figuraliter* often extend beyond figural prophecy. Tertullian uses *allegoria* almost synonymously with *figura,* though much less frequently, and in Arnobius (*Adversus nationes* 5, 32; *Patrologia Latina,* Vol. 53, col. 1147) we find *historia* opposed to *allegoria; allegoria* also benefited by the authority of Gal. 4:24. But *allegoria* could not be used synonymously with *figura* in all contexts, for it did not have the same implication of "form"; one could not write that *Adam est allegoria Christi.* As for *typus,* the only reason why it fell behind *figura* is that it was a foreign word. But this consideration was far from negligible, for in anyone who spoke Latin (or later a Romance language), *figura* more or less consciously evoked all the notions involved in its history, while *typus* remained an imported, lifeless sign. As for the Latin words which were, or at least could be employed for prefiguration in place of *figura,* they are as follows: *ambages, effigies, exemplum, imago, similitudo, species,* and *umbra. Ambages* was dropped as too pejorative; *effigies* in the sense of "copy" was too narrow, and even in comparison with *imago,* seems to have developed little power of expansion; the others cut across the meaning of "figural prophecy" in various ways, but do not fully satisfy it. They are all used occasionally, the most frequent being *imago* and *umbra. Imagines,* absolute and without a genitive, was employed for the statues of ancestors in Roman houses; in Christian usage they became the pictures and statues of the saints, so that the meaning developed in a different direction; nevertheless, according to the Vulgate, man was made *ad imaginem Dei* ("in the image of God"), and consequently *imago* long competed with *figura,* though only in passages where the context made the meaning "image" identical with "prefiguration." *Umbra* was supported chiefly by a few passages in the Pauline Epistles (Col. 2:17; Heb. 8:5 and 10:1); it occurs frequently, but more as a metaphoric turn for

figura than as a direct designation. In any event, none
of these words combined the elements of the concept
so fully as *figura:* the creative, formative principle,
change amid the enduring essence, the shades of
meaning between copy and archetype. Hence it is not
surprising that *figura* should have been most often
and most widely used for this purpose.

III. Origin and Analysis of Figural Interpretation

In the last section we involuntarily digressed several
times from our purely semantic discussion, because
the idea which the word expresses in the Church
Fathers is itself in need of explanation. It thus becomes necessary to investigate the origins of this idea
in greater detail, to distinguish it from related ideas,
and to examine its historical destinies and influence.

The Church Fathers often justify the figural interpretation on the basis of certain passages in early
Christian writings, mostly from the Pauline Epistles.[33]
The most important of these is I Cor. 10:6 and 11,
where the Jews in the desert are termed *typoi hēmōn*
("figures of ourselves"), and where it is written that
tauta de typikōs synebainen ekeinois ("these things
befell them as figures"). Another passage often ad-
duced is Gal. 4:21-31, where Paul explains to the
freshly baptized Galatians, who, still under the influence of Judaism, wished to be circumcised, the difference between law and grace, the old and the new
covenant, servitude and freedom, by the example of
Hagar-Ishmael and Sarah-Isaac, linking the narrative
in Genesis with Is. 54:1 and interpreting it in terms
of figural prophecy. Still others are Col. 2:16 f., saying that the Jewish dietary laws and holidays are only
the shadow of things to come, whereas the body is

Christ; Rom. 5:12 ff. and I Cor. 15:21, where Adam appears as the *typos* of the future Christ, and grace is opposed to the law; II Cor. 3:14, which speaks of the veil (*kalymnos*) that covers the Scripture when the Jews read it; and finally Heb. 9:11 ff., where the sacrifice of Christ's blood is represented as the fulfillment of the high priest's sacrifice in the Old Testament.

Certain passages in Acts (e.g., 8:32) show that figural interpretation played an important part in the Christian mission from the very start. It seems only natural that the new Judaeo-Christians should have looked for prefigurations and confirmations of Jesus in the Old Testament and incorporated the interpretations thus arrived at into the tradition; particularly since the notion was current among them that the Messiah would be a second Moses, that his redemption would be a second exodus from Egypt in which the miracles of the first would be repeated.[34] This would require no further explanation. But an examination of the above-cited passages, particularly if they are considered in connection with Paul's preaching as a whole, shows that in him these Jewish conceptions were combined with a pronounced hostility to the ideas of the Judaeo-Christians, and that it is this attitude which gives them their special significance. Those passages in the Pauline Epistles which contain figural interpretations were almost all written in the course of Paul's bitter struggle in behalf of his mission among the Gentiles; many are answers to the attacks and persecutions of the Judaeo-Christians; nearly all are intended to strip the Old Testament of its normative character and show that it is merely a shadow of things to come. His whole figural interpretation was subordinated to the basic Pauline theme of grace versus law, faith versus works: the old law is an-

nulled; it is shadow and *typos;* observance of it has
become useless and even harmful since Christ made
his sacrifice; a Christian is justified not by works in
observance of the law, but by faith; and in its Jewish
and Judaistic legal sense the Old Testament is the
letter that kills, while the new Christians are servants
of the new covenant, of the spirit that gives life. This
was Paul's doctrine, and the former Pharisee and
disciple of Gamaliel looked eagerly in the Old Testament for passages in support of it. As a whole it
ceased for him to be a book of the law and history
of Israel and became from beginning to end a promise
and prefiguration of Christ, in which there is no definitive, but only a prophetic meaning which has now
been fulfilled, in which everything is written "for our
sakes" (I Cor. 9:10, cf. Rom. 15:4) and in which precisely the most important and sacred events, sacraments and laws are provisional forms and figurations
of Christ and the Gospel: *etenim Pascha nostrum
immolatus est Christi* (I Cor. 5:7) ("for even Christ
our passover is sacrificed for us").[35]

In this way his thinking, which eminently combined practical politics with creative poetic faith,
transformed the Jewish conception of Moses risen
again in the Messiah into a system of figural prophecy,
in which the risen one both fulfills and annuls the
work of his precursor. What the Old Testament
thereby lost as a book of national history, it gained in
concrete dramatic actuality. Paul devised no systematic
interpretation of the Old Testament, but the few
passages about the Exodus, about Adam and Christ,
Hagar and Sarah, etc., show sufficiently what his intention was. The Old Testament controversies of the
ensuing period kept his conception and interpretation
alive; true, the influence of the Judaeo-Christians with
their fidelity to the law soon diminished, but a new

opposition came from those who wished either to exclude the Old Testament altogether or to interpret it only abstractly and allegorically—whereby Christianity would necessarily have lost its conception of a providential history, its intrinsic concreteness, and with these no doubt some of its immense persuasive power. In the struggle against those who despised the Old Testament and tried to despoil it of its meaning, the figural method again proved its worth.

In this connection we should bear in mind another factor which became important as Christianity spread through the countries of the western and northern Mediterranean. As we have seen, the figural interpretation changed the Old Testament from a book of laws and a history of the people of Israel into a series of figures of Christ and the Redemption, such as we find later in the procession of prophets in the medieval theater and in the cyclic representations of medieval sculpture. In this form and in this context, from which Jewish history and national character had vanished, the Celtic and Germanic peoples, for example, could accept the Old Testament; it was a part of the universal religion of salvation and a necessary component of the equally magnificent and universal vision of history that was conveyed to them along with this religion. In its original form, as law book and history of so foreign and remote a nation, it would have been beyond their reach. This of course was a later insight, far from the thoughts of the first preachers to the Gentiles and of the Church Fathers. The problem did not arise in the early period, for the first pagan converts lived among the Jews of the Diaspora, and what with the important influence of the Jews and the receptivity of the Hellenistic world of that time to religious experience, they had long been familiar with Jewish history and religion. But the fact that we can only discern it in retrospect does not make this consideration any less important. It was not until very late, probably not until after the Reformation, that Europeans began to regard the Old Testament as Jewish history and Jewish law; it first came to the newly converted peoples as *figura rerum* or phenomenal prophecy, as a prefiguration of Christ, so giving them a basic conception of history, which derived its compelling force from its inseparable bond with the faith, and which for almost a thousand years remained the only accepted view of history. Consequently the attitude embodied in the figural interpretation became one of the essential elements of the Christian picture of reality, history, and the concrete world in general. This consideration leads us to the second of the tasks we set ourselves at the beginning of this chapter, namely to define figural interpretation more sharply and to distinguish it from other, related forms of interpretation.

Figural interpretation establishes a connection between two events or persons, the first of which signifies not only itself but also the second, while the second encompasses or fulfills the first. The two poles of the figure are separate in time, but both, being real events or figures, are within time, within the stream of historical life. Only the understanding of the two persons or events is a spiritual act, but this spiritual act deals with concrete events whether past, present, or future, and not with concepts or abstractions; these are quite secondary, since promise and fulfillment are real historical events, which have either happened in the incarnation of the Word, or will happen in the second coming. Of course purely spiritual elements enter into the conceptions of the ultimate fulfillment, since "my kingdom is not of this world"; yet it will be a real kingdom, not an immaterial abstraction;

only the *figura,* not the *natura* of this world will pass away (see above p. 37), and the flesh will rise again. Since in figural interpretation one thing stands for another, since one thing represents and signifies the other, figural interpretation is "allegorical" in the widest sense. But it differs from most of the allegorical forms known to us by the historicity both of the sign and what it signifies. Most of the allegories we find in literature or art represent a virtue (e.g., wisdom), or a passion (jealousy), an institution (justice), or at most a very general synthesis of historical phenomena (peace, the fatherland)—never a definite event in its full historicity. Such are the allegories of late antiquity and the Middle Ages, extending roughly from the *Psychomachia*[36] of Prudentius to Alain de Lille and the *Roman de la Rose*. We find something very similar (or diametrically opposite if one prefers) in the allegorical interpretations of historical events,[37] which were usually interpreted as obscure illustrations of philosophical doctrines. In biblical exegesis this allegorical method long competed with the figural interpretation; it was the method of Philo[38] and the catechetical school of Alexandria, which was under his influence. It was rooted in a much older tradition. Various philosophical schools had long interpreted the Greek myths, particularly Homer and Hesiod, as veiled expositions of their own physico-cosmological system. And various later influences, no longer purely rationalistic but more mystical and religious, were also at work. All the numerous sects and occult doctrines of late antiquity cultivated the allegorical interpretation of myths, signs, and texts, and in their interpretations the physical and cosmological aspect gradually gave way to the ethical and mystical. Philo himself, who in keeping with the Jewish tradition constructed his philosophy as a commentary on Scripture, interpreted the various events of the Bible as phases in the development of the soul and its relation to the intelligible world; in the destinies of Israel as a whole and of the protagonists of Jewish history, he saw an allegory of the movement of the sinful soul in need of salvation, its fall, hope, and ultimate redemption. This clearly spiritual and extrahistorical form of interpretation enjoyed great influence in late antiquity, in part because it was merely the most respectable manifestation of an immense spiritualist movement centered in Alexandria; not only texts and events, but also natural phenomena, stars, animals, stones, were stripped of their concrete reality and interpreted allegorically or on occasion somewhat figurally. The spiritualist-ethical-allegorical method was taken up by the catechetical school of Alexandria and found its outstanding Christian exponent in Origen. As we know, it continued into the Middle Ages side by side with the figural method. But despite the existence of numerous hybrid forms, it is very different from figural interpretation. It too transforms the Old Testament; in it too the law and history of Israel lose their national and popular character; but these are replaced by a mystical or ethical system, and the text loses far more of its concrete history than in the figural system. This type of exegesis long maintained its position; in the doctrine of the fourfold meaning of Scripture, it wholly determined one of the four meanings, the ethical, and partly accounted for another, the analogical. And yet I believe, though I can offer no strict proof of it, that independently, that is to say, without the support of the figural method, it would have had little influence on the freshly converted peoples. There is something scholarly, indirect, even abstruse about it, except on the rare occasions when a gifted mystic breathes force into it. By its origin and nature,

it was limited to a relatively small circle of intellectu-
als and initiates; they alone could find pleasure and
nourishment in it. Figural phenomenal prophecy,
however, had grown out of a definite historical situation, the Christian break with Judaism and the
Christian mission among the Gentiles; it had a historical function. Its integral, firmly teleological view
of history and the providential order of the world
gave it the power to capture the imagination and in-
nermost feeling of the convert nations. By its success
it paved the way for less concrete schools of allegorism,
such as that of the Alexandrians. But although this
and other spiritualistic methods of interpretation may
be older than the figural method of the apostles and
Church Fathers, they are unmistakably late forms,
while the figural interpretation with its living historicity, though scarcely primitive or archaic, was
assuredly a fresh beginning and rebirth of man's
creative powers.

Aside from the allegorical form we have just been
discussing there are still other ways of representing
one thing by another that may be compared with
figural prophecy: namely the so-called symbolic or
mythical forms, which are often regarded as characteristic of primitive cultures, and which in any case are
often found in them; so much material concerning
these forms has been brought to light in recent years,
and the process of sifting and explaining this material
is so far from complete that we can speak of them
only with caution. These forms were first recognized
and described by Vico. Their characteristic feature is
that the thing represented must always be something
very important and holy for those concerned, something affecting their whole life and thinking, and that
this something is not only expressed or imitated in
the sign or symbol, but considered to be itself present

and contained in it. Thus the symbol itself can act and be acted upon in its place; to act upon the symbol is conceived as tantamount to acting on the thing symbolized, and consequently magical powers are imputed to the symbol. Such symbolic or mythical forms still existed in the Mediterranean countries in late antiquity, but for the most part they had lost their magical force and had paled to allegory; very much as vestiges of them, the symbols of justice in heraldry and national emblems, for example, have lived on in our modern cultures, though on the other hand, as we may observe, both in late antiquity and in modern times, new ideas of universal appeal never cease to create symbols which act as magical realities. These symbolic or mythical forms have certain points of contact with the figural interpretation; both aspire to interpret and order life as a whole; both are conceivable only in religious or related spheres. But the differences are self-evident. The symbol must possess magic power, not the *figura;* the *figura,* on the other hand, must always be historical, but not the symbol. Of course Christianity has no lack of magic symbols; but the *figura* as such is not one of them.[39] What actually makes the two forms completely different is that figural prophecy relates to an interpretation of history —indeed it is by nature a textual interpretation— while the symbol is a direct interpretation of life and originally no doubt for the most part, of nature. Thus figural interpretation is a product of late cultures, far more indirect, complex, and charged with history than the symbol or myth. Indeed, seen from this point of view, it has something vastly old about it: a great culture had to reach its culmination and indeed to show signs of old age, before an interpretive tradition could produce something on the order of figural prophecy.

These two comparisons, with allegory on the one hand and with the symbolical, mythical forms on the other, disclose figural prophecy in a twofold light: youthful and newborn as a purposive, creative, concrete interpretation of universal history; infinitely old as the late interpretation of a venerable text, charged with history, that had grown for hundreds of years. Its youthful vitality gave it the almost unequalled persuasive power with which it captivated not only the late cultures of the Mediterranean, but also the relatively youthful peoples of the West and North; what was old in it gave the thinking of those peoples and their understanding of history a peculiarly puzzling quality, which we shall now attempt to elucidate. Figural prophecy implies the interpretation of one worldly event through another; the first signifies the second, the second fulfills the first. Both remain historical events; yet both, looked at in this way, have something provisional and incomplete about them; they point to one another and both point to something in the future, something still to come, which will be the actual, real, and definitive event. This is true not only of Old Testament prefiguration, which points forward to the incarnation and the proclamation of the gospel, but also of these latter events, for they too are not the ultimate fulfillment, but themselves a promise of the end of time and the true kingdom of God. Thus history, with all its concrete force, remains forever a figure, cloaked and needful of interpretation. In this light the history of no epoch ever has the practical self-sufficiency which, from the standpoint both of primitive man and of modern science, resides in the accomplished fact; all history, rather, remains open and questionable, points to something still concealed, and the tentativeness of events in the figural interpretation is fundamentally different from

the tentativeness of events in the modern view of
historical development. In the modern view, the provisional event is treated as a step in an unbroken hori-
zontal process; in the figural system the interpretation
is always sought from above; events are considered not
in their unbroken relation to one another, but torn
apart, individually, each in relation to something
other that is promised and not yet present. Whereas
in the modern view the event is always self-sufficient
and secure, while the interpretation is fundamentally
incomplete, in the figural interpretation the fact is
subordinated to an interpretation which is fully secured to begin with: the event is enacted according to
an ideal model which is a prototype situated in the
future and thus far only promised. This model situated in the future and imitated in the figures (one is
reminded of the term *imitatio veritatis* ["imitation of
the truth"], p. 44 above) recalls Platonistic notions. It
carries us still further. For every future model, though
incomplete as history, is already fulfilled in God and
has existed from all eternity in His providence. The
figures in which He cloaked it, and the incarnation in
which He revealed its meaning, are therefore prophecies of something that has always been, but which
will remain veiled for men until the day when they
behold the Saviour *revelata facie,* with the senses as
well as in spirit. Thus the figures are not only tentative; they are also the tentative form of something
eternal and timeless; they point not only to the concrete future, but also to something that always has
been and always will be; they point to something
which is in need of interpretation, which will indeed
be fulfilled in the concrete future, but which is at all
times present, fulfilled in God's providence, which
knows no difference of time. This eternal thing is already figured in them, and thus they are both tenta-

tive fragmentary reality, and veiled eternal reality. This becomes eminently clear in the sacrament of the sacrifice, the Last Supper, the *pascha nostrum,* which is *figura Christi.*[40]

This sacrament, which is figure as well as symbol, and which has long existed historically—namely, since it was first established in the old covenant—gives us the purest picture of the concretely present, the veiled and tentative, the eternal and supratemporal elements contained in the figures.

IV. Figural Art in the Middle Ages

The figural interpretation, or to put it more completely, the figural view of history was widespread and deeply influential up to the Middle Ages, and beyond. This has not escaped the attention of scholars. Not only theological works on the history of hermeneutics but also studies on the history of art and literature have met with figural conceptions on their way, and dealt with them. This is particularly true of the history of art in connection with medieval iconography, and of the history of literature in connection with the religious theater of the Middle Ages. But the special nature of the problem does not seem to have been recognized; the figural or typological or phenomenal structure is not sharply distinguished from other, allegorical or symbolical, forms. A beginning is to be found in T. C. Goode's instructive dissertation on Gonzalo de Berceo's *El Sacrificio de la Misa* (Washington, 1933); although he does not go into fundamental questions, H. Pflaum shows a clear understanding of the situation in his *Die religiose Disputation in der europäischen Dichtung des Mittelalters* (Geneva-Florence, 1935). Recently (in *Ro-*

mania, LXIII) his sound understanding of the word *figure* enabled him to give a correct interpretation of some Old French verses that had been misunderstood by the editor and to restore the text. Perhaps other examples have escaped me,[41] but I do not think that there is any systematic treatment of the subject. Yet such an investigation strikes me as indispensable for an understanding of the mixture of spirituality and sense of reality which characterizes the European Middle Ages and which seems so baffling to us.[42] In most European countries figural interpretation was active up to the eighteenth century; we find traces of it not only in Bossuet as might be expected, but many years later in the religious authors whom Groethuysen quotes in *Les Origines de la France bourgeoise.*[43] A clear knowledge of its character and how it differed from related but differently structured forms would generally sharpen and deepen our understanding of the documents of late antiquity and the Middle Ages, and solve a good many puzzles. Might the themes that recur so frequently on early Christian sarcophagi and in the catacombs not be figures of the Resurrection? Or to cite an example from Mâle's great work, might not the legend of Maria Aegyptiaca, the representations of which in the Toulouse Museum he describes (op. cit., p. 240 ff.), be a figure of the people of Israel going out of Egypt, hence to be interpreted exactly as the Psalm *In exitu Israel de Aegypto* was generally interpreted in the Middle Ages?

But individual interpretations do not exhaust the importance of the figural method. No student of the Middle Ages can fail to see how it provides the medieval interpretation of history with its general foundation and often enters into the medieval view of everyday reality. The analogism that reaches into every sphere of medieval thought is closely bound up

with the figural structure; in the interpretation of
the Trinity that extends roughly from Augustine's *De
Trinitate* to St. Thomas, I, q. 45, art. 7, man himself,
as the image of God, takes on the character of a
figura Trinitatis. It is not quite clear to me how far
aesthetic ideas were determined by figural conceptions—to what extent the work of art was viewed as
the *figura* of a still unattainable fulfillment in reality.
The question of the imitation of nature in art aroused
little theoretical interest in the Middle Ages; but all
the more attention was accorded to the notion that the
artist, as a kind of figure for God the Creator, realized
an archetype that was alive in his spirit.[44] These, as
we see, are ideas of Neoplatonic origin. But the question remains: to what extent were this archetype and
the work of art produced from it regarded as figures
for a reality and truth fulfilled in God? I have found
no conclusive answer in the texts available to me here
and the most important works of the specialized literature are lacking. But I should like to quote a few
passages which happen to be at hand, and which point
somewhat in the direction I have in mind. In an
article on the representation of musical tones in the
capitals of the Abbey of Cluny (*Deutsche Vierteljahrsschrift,* 7, p. 264) L. Schrade quotes an explanation of the word *imitari* by Remigius of Auxerre:
*scilicet persequi, quia veram musicam non potest hu-
mana musica imitari* ("that is, to follow after, for the
music of man cannot imitate the true music"). This is
probably based on the notion that the artist's work is
an imitation or at least a shadowy figuration of a true
and likewise sensuous reality (the music of the heavenly choirs). In the *Purgatorio* Dante praises the works
of art created by God himself, representing examples
of virtues and vices, for their perfectly fulfilled sensuous truth, beside which human art and even nature

pales (*Purg.,* 10 and 12); his invocation to Apollo (*Par.,* 1) includes the lines:

> *O divina virtù, se mi ti presti*
> *tanto che l'ombra del beato regno*
> *segnata nel mio capo io manifesti*

(O divine Virtue, if thou dost so far lend thyself to me, that I make manifest the shadow of the blessed realm imprinted on my brain.) (Temple Classics ed., p. 5.)

Here his poetry is characterized as an *umbra* of truth, engraved in his mind, and his theory of inspiration is sometimes expressed in statements that may be explained along the same lines. But these are only suggestions; an investigation purporting to explain the relation between Neoplatonic and figural elements in medieval aesthetics would require broader foundations. Still, the present remarks suffice, I believe, to show the need for distinguishing the figural structure from the other forms of imagery. We may say roughly that the figural method in Europe goes back to Christian influences, while the allegorical method derives from ancient pagan sources, and also that the one is applied primarily to Christian, the other to ancient material. Nor shall we be going too far afield in terming the figural view the predominantly Christian-medieval one, while the allegorical view, modeled on pagan or not inwardly Christianized authors of late antiquity, tends to appear where ancient, pagan, or strongly secular influences are dominant. But such observations are too general and imprecise, for the many phenomena that reflect an intermingling of different cultures over a thousand years do not admit of such simple classifications. At a very early date profane and pagan material was also interpreted figurally;

Gregory of Tours, for example, uses the legend of the
Seven Sleepers as a figure for the Resurrection; the
waking of Lazarus from the dead and Jonah's rescue
from the belly of the whale were also commonly interpreted in this sense. In the high Middle Ages, the
Sybils, Virgil, the characters of the *Aeneid,* and even
those of the Breton legend cycle (e.g., Galahad in the
quest for the Holy Grail) were drawn into the figural
interpretation, and moreover there were all sorts of
mixtures between figural, allegoric, and symbolic
forms. All these forms, applied to classical as well as
Christian material, occur in the work which concludes
and sums up the culture of the Middle Ages: the
Divine Comedy. But I shall now attempt to show
that basically it is the figural forms which predominate
and determine the whole structure of the poem.

At the foot of the mountain of Purgatory, Dante
and Virgil meet a man of venerable mien, whose
countenance is illumined by four stars signifying the
four cardinal virtues. He inquires sternly into the
legitimacy of their journey and from Virgil's re-
spectful reply—after he has told Dante to kneel before this man—we learn that it is Cato of Utica. For
after explaining his divine mission, Virgil continues
as follows (*Purg.,* 1, 70-5):

> *Or ti piaccia gradir la sua venuta.*
> *libertà va cercando, che è sì cara,*
> *come sa chi per lei vita rifiuta.*
> *Tu il sai, chè non ti fu per lei amara*
> *in Utica la morte, ove lasciasti*
> *la vesta che al gran dì sarà sì chiara.*

(Now may it please thee to be gracious unto his coming: he seeketh freedom, which is so precious, as he
knows who giveth up life for her.

Thou knowest it; since for her sake death was not

bitter to thee in Utica, where thou leftest the raiment
which at the great day shall be so bright.)

(Temple Classics ed., p. 7.)

Virgil goes on, asking Cato to favor him for the sake
of the memory of Marcia, his former wife. This plea
Cato rejects with undiminished severity; but if such
is the desire of the *donna del ciel* (Beatrice), that
suffices; and he orders that before his ascent Dante's
face be cleansed of the stains of Hell and that he be
girded with reeds. Cato appears again at the end of
the second canto, where he sternly rebukes the souls
just arrived at the foot of the mountain, who are
listening in self-forgetfulness to Casella's song, and
reminds them to get on with their journey.

It is Cato of Utica whom God has here appointed
guardian at the foot of Purgatory: a pagan, an enemy
of Caesar, and a suicide. This is startling, and the
very first commentators, such as Benvenuto of Imola,
expressed their bewilderment. Dante mentions only a
very few pagans who were freed from Hell by Christ;
and among them we find an enemy of Caesar, whose
associates, Caesar's murderers, are with Judas in the
jaws of Lucifer, who as a suicide seems no less guilty
than those others "who have done themselves violence" and who for the same sin are suffering the most
frightful torments in the seventh circle of Hell. The
riddle is solved by the words of Virgil, who says that
Dante is seeking freedom, which is so precious as you
yourself know who have despised life for its sake. The
story of Cato is removed from its earthly and political
context, just as the stories of Isaac, Jacob, etc., were
removed from theirs by the patristic exegetes of the
Old Testament, and made into a *figura futurorum.*
Cato is a *figura,* or rather the earthly Cato, who re-
nounced his life for freedom, was a *figura,* and the

Cato who appears here in the *Purgatorio* is the revealed or fulfilled figure, the truth of that figural event. The political and earthly freedom for which he died was only an *umbra futurorum:* a prefiguration of the Christian freedom whose guardian he is here appointed, and for the sake of which he here again opposes all earthly temptation; the Christian freedom from all evil impulses, which leads to true domination of self, the freedom for the acquisition of which Dante is girded with the rushes of humility, until, on the summit of the mountain, he actually achieves it and is crowned by Virgil as lord over himself. Cato's voluntary choice of death rather than political servitude is here introduced as a *figura* for the eternal freedom of the children of God, in behalf of which all earthly things are to be despised, for the liberation of the soul from the servitude of sin. Dante's choice of Cato for this role is explained by the position "above the parties" that Cato occupies according to the Roman authors, who held him up as a model of virtue, justice, piety, and love of freedom. Dante found him praised equally in Cicero, Virgil, Lucan, Seneca, and Valerius Maximus; particularly Virgil's *secretosque pios his dantem iura Catonem (Aeneid,* 8, 670) ("the righteous in a place apart, with Cato their lawgiver"), coming as it did from a poet of the Empire, must have made a great impression on him. His admiration for Cato may be judged from several passages in the *Convivio,* and in his *De Monarchia* (2, 5) he has a quotation from Cicero[45] saying that Cato's voluntary death should be judged in a special light and connecting it with the examples of Roman political virtue to which Dante attached so much importance; in this passage Dante tries to show that Roman rule was legitimized by Roman virtue; that it fostered the justice and freedom of all mankind. The chapter contains this sentence: *Romanum imperium de fonte nascitur pietatis* ("the Roman Empire springs from the fount of justice").[46]

Dante believed in a predetermined concordance between the Christian story of salvation and the Roman secular monarchy; thus it is not surprising that he should apply the figural interpretation to a pagan Roman—in general he draws his symbols, allegories, and figures from both worlds without distinction. Beyond any doubt Cato is a *figura;* not an allegory like the characters from the *Roman de la Rose,* but a figure that has become the truth. The *Comedy* is a vision which regards and proclaims the figural truth as already fulfilled, and what constitutes its distinctive character is precisely that, fully in the spirit of figural interpretation, it attaches the truth perceived in the vision to historical, earthly events. The character of Cato as a severe, righteous, and pious man, who in a significant moment in his own destiny and in the providential history of the world sets freedom above life, is preserved in its full historical and personal force; it does not become an allegory for freedom; no, Cato of Utica stands there as a unique individual, just as Dante saw him; but he is lifted out of the tentative earthly state in which he regarded political freedom as the highest good (just as the Jews singled out strict observance of the Law), and transposed into a state of definitive fulfillment, concerned no longer with the earthly works of civic virtue or the law, but with the *ben dell'intelletto,* the highest good, the freedom of the immortal soul in the sight of God.

Let us attempt the same demonstration in a somewhat more difficult case. Virgil has been taken by almost all commentators as an allegory for reason— the human, natural reason which leads to the right earthly order, that is, in Dante's view, the secular monarchy. The older commentators had no objection to a purely allegorical interpretation, for they did not, as we do today, feel that allegory was incompatible with authentic poetry. Many modern critics have argued against this idea, stressing the poetic, human, personal quality of Dante's Virgil; still, they have been unable either to deny that he "means something" or to find a satisfactory relation between this meaning and the human reality. Recently (and not only in connection with Virgil) a number of writers (L. Valli and Mandonnet, for example) have gone back to the purely allegorical or symbolic aspect and attempted to reject the historical reality as "positivistic" or "romantic." But actually there is no choice between historical and hidden meaning; both are present. The figural structure preserves the historical event while interpreting it as revelation; and must preserve it in order to interpret it.

In Dante's eyes the historical Virgil is both poet and guide. He is a poet and a guide because in the righteous Aeneas' journey to the underworld he prophesies and glorifies universal peace under the Roman Empire, the political order which Dante regards as exemplary, as the *terrena Jerusalem;*[47] and because in his poem the founding of Rome, predestined seat of the secular and spiritual power, is celebrated in the light of its future mission. Above all he is poet and guide because all the great poets who came after him have been inflamed and inspired by his work; Dante not only states this for himself, but brings in a second poet, Statius, to proclaim the same thing most emphatically: in the meeting with Sordello and perhaps also in the highly controversial verse about Guido Cavalcanti (*Inf.,* 10, 63) the same theme is sounded. In addition, Virgil is a guide because, beyond his

temporal prophecy, he also—in the Fourth Eclogue—
proclaimed the eternal transcendent order, the appearance of Christ which would usher in the renewal
of the temporal world without, to be sure, suspecting
the significance of his own words, but nevertheless in
such a way that posterity might derive inspiration
from his light. Virgil the poet was a guide because he
had described the realm of the dead—thus he knew
the way thither. But also as a Roman and a man, he
was destined to be a guide, for not only was he a
master of eloquent discourse and lofty wisdom but
also possessed the qualities that fit a man for guidance
and leadership, the qualities that characterize his hero
Aeneas and Rome in general: *iustitia* and *pietas*. For
Dante the historical Virgil embodied this fullness of
earthly perfection and was therefore capable of guid-
ing him to the very threshold of insight into the divine and eternal perfection; the historic Virgil was for
him a *figura* of the poet-prophet-guide, now fulfilled
in the other world. The historical Virgil is "fulfilled"
by the dweller in limbo, the companion of the great
poets of antiquity, who at the wish of Beatrice under-
takes to guide Dante. As a Roman and poet Virgil had
sent Aeneas down to the underworld in search of
divine counsel to learn the destiny of the Roman
world; and now Virgil is summoned by the heavenly
powers to exercise a no less important guidance; for
there is no doubt that Dante saw himself in a mission
no less important than that of Aeneas: elected to di-
vulge to a world out of joint the right order, which
is revealed to him upon his way. Virgil is elected to
point out and interpret for him the true earthly order,
whose laws are carried out and whose essence is fulfilled in the other world, and at the same time to direct him toward its goal, the heavenly community of
the blessed, which he has presaged in his poetry—yet

not into the heart of the kingdom of God, for the
meaning of his presage was not revealed to him during
his earthly lifetime, and without such illumination he
has died an unbeliever. Thus God does not wish
Dante to enter His kingdom with Virgil's help; Virgil
can lead him only to the threshold of the kingdom,
only as far as the limit which his noble and righteous
poetry was able to discern. "Thou first," says Statius
to Virgil, "didst send me towards Parnassus to drink
in its caves, and then didst light me on to God. Thou
didst like one who goes by night, and carries the
light behind him, and profits not himself, but maketh
persons wise that follow him. . . . Through thee I
was a poet, through thee a Christian." [48] And just as
the earthly Virgil led Statius to salvation, so now, as
a fulfilled figure, he leads Dante: for Dante too has
received from him the lofty style of poetry, through
him he is saved from eternal damnation and set on the
way of salvation; and just as he once illumined
Statius, without himself seeing the light that he bore
and proclaimed, so now he leads Dante to the threshold of the light, which he knows of, but may not himself behold.

Thus Virgil is not an allegory of an attribute, virtue, capacity, power, or historical institution. He is
neither reason nor poetry nor the Empire. He is
Virgil himself. Yet he is not himself in the same way
as the historical characters whom later poets have
set out to portray in all their historical involvement,
as for example, Shakespeare's Caesar or Schiller's Wall-
enstein. These poets disclose their historical characters
in the thick of their earthly existence; they bring an
important epoch to life before our eyes, and look
for the meaning of the epoch itself. For Dante the
meaning of every life has its place in the providential
history of the world, the general lines of which are

laid down in the Revelation which has been given to every Christian, and which is interpreted for him in the vision of the *Comedy*. Thus Virgil in the *Divine Comedy* is the historical Virgil himself, but then again he is not; for the historical Virgil is only a *figura* of the fulfilled truth that the poem reveals, and this fulfillment is more real, more significant than the *figura*. With Dante, unlike modern poets, the more fully the figure is interpreted and the more closely it is integrated with the eternal plan of salvation, the more real it becomes. And for him, unlike the ancient poets of the underworld, who represented earthly life as real and the life after death as shadow, for him the other world is the true reality, while this world is only *umbra futurorum*—though indeed the *umbra* is the prefiguration of the transcendent reality and must recur fully in it.

For what has been said here of Cato and Virgil applies to the *Comedy* as a whole. It is wholly based on a figural conception. In my study of Dante as a poet of the earthly world (1929) I attempted to show that in the *Comedy* Dante undertook "to conceive the whole earthly historical world . . . as already subjected to God's final judgment and thus put in its proper place as decreed by the divine judgment, to represent it as a world already judged . . . in so doing, he does not destroy or weaken the earthly nature of his characters, but captures the fullest intensity of their individual earthly-historical being and identifies it with the ultimate state of things" (p. 108). At that time I lacked a solid historical grounding for this view, which is already to be found in Hegel and which is the basis of my interpretation of the *Divine Comedy;* it is suggested rather than formulated in the introductory chapters of the book. I believe that I have now found this historical grounding; it is precisely the figural interpretation of reality which, though in constant conflict with purely spiritualist and Neoplatonic tendencies, was the dominant view in the European Middle Ages: the idea that earthly life is thoroughly real, with the reality of the flesh into which the Logos entered, but that with all its reality it is only *umbra* and *figura* of the authentic, future, ultimate truth, the real reality that will unveil and preserve the *figura*. In this way the individual earthly event is not regarded as a definitive self-sufficient reality, nor as a link in a chain of development in which single events or combinations of events perpetually give rise to new events, but viewed primarily in immediate vertical connection with a divine order which encompasses it, which on some future day will itself be concrete reality; so that the earthly event is a prophecy or *figura* of a part of a wholly divine reality that will be enacted in the future. But this reality is not only future; it is always present in the eye of God and in the other world, which is to say that in transcendence the revealed and true reality is present at all times, or timelessly. Dante's work is an attempt to give a poetic and at the same time systematic picture of the world in this light. Divine grace comes to the help of a man menaced by earthly confusion and ruin—this is the framework of the vision. From early youth he had been favored by special grace, because he was destined for a special task; at an early age he had been privileged to see revelation incarnated in a living being, Beatrice—and here as so often figural structure and Neoplatonism are intertwined. In her lifetime she had, though covertly, favored him with a salutation of her eyes and mouth; and in dying she had distinguished him in an unspoken mysterious way.[49] When he strays from the right path, the departed Beatrice, who for him was revelation incarnate, finds the only possible salvation for him; indirectly she is his guide and in Paradise directly; it is she who shows him the unveiled order, the truth of the earthly figures. What he sees and learns in the three realms is true, concrete reality, in which the earthly *figura* is contained and interpreted; by seeing the fulfilled truth while still alive, he himself is saved, while at the same time he is enabled to tell the world what he has seen and guide it to the right path.

Insight into the figural character of the *Comedy* does not offer a universal method by which to interpret every controversial passage; but we can derive certain principles of interpretation from it. We may be certain that every historical or mythical character occurring in the poem can only mean something closely connected with what Dante knew of his historical or mythical existence, and that the relation is one of fulfillment and figure; we must always be careful not to deny their earthly historical existence altogether, not to confine ourselves to an abstract, allegorical interpretation. This applies particularly to Beatrice. The romantic realism of the nineteenth century overemphasized the human Beatrice, tending to make the *Vita Nova* a kind of sentimental novel. Since then a reaction has set in; the new tendency is to do away with her entirely, to dissolve her in an assortment of increasingly subtle theological concepts. But actually there is no reality in such a choice. For Dante the literal meaning or historical reality of a figure stands in no contradiction to its profounder meaning, but precisely "figures" it; the historical reality is not annulled, but confirmed and fulfilled by the deeper meaning. The Beatrice of the *Vita Nova* is an earthly person; she really appeared to Dante, she really saluted him, really withheld her salutation later on, mocked him, mourned for a dead friend and for her father, and really died. Of course this reality can only be the reality of Dante's experience—for a poet forms and transforms the events of his life in his consciousness, and we can take account only of what lived in his consciousness and not of the outward reality. It should also be borne in mind that from the first day of her appearance the earthly Beatrice was for Dante a miracle sent from Heaven, an incarnation of divine truth. Thus the reality of her earthly person is not, as in the case of Virgil or Cato, derived from the facts of a historic tradition, but from Dante's own experience: this experience showed him the earthly Beatrice as a miracle.[50] But an incarnation, a miracle are real happenings; miracles happen on earth, and incarnation is flesh. The strangeness of the medieval view of reality has prevented modern scholars from distinguishing between figuration and allegory and led them for the most part to perceive only the latter.[51] Even so acute a theological critic as Mandonnet (op. cit., pp. 218-19) considers only two possibilities: either Beatrice is a mere allegory (and this is his opinion) or she is *la petite Bice Portinari,* a notion that he ridicules. Quite aside from the misunderstanding of poetic reality that such a judgment shows, it is surprising to find so deep a chasm between reality and meaning. Is the *terrena Jerusalem* without historical reality because it is a *figura aeternae Jerusalem?*

In the *Vita Nova,* then, Beatrice is a living woman from the reality of Dante's experience—and in the *Comedy* she is no *intellectus separatus,* no angel, but a blessed human being who will rise again in the flesh at the Last Judgment. Actually there is no dogmatic concept that would wholly describe her; certain events in the *Vita Nova* would not fit into any allegory, and in regard to the *Comedy* there is the additional problem of drawing an exact distinction between her and various other persons of the *Paradiso*, such as the Apostle-Examiners and St. Bernard. Nor can the special character of her relation to Dante be fully understood in this way. Most of the older commentators interpreted Beatrice as theology; more recent ones have sought subtler formulations; but this has led to exaggeration and mistakes: even Mandonnet, who applies to Beatrice the extremely broad notion of *ordre surnaturel,* derived from the contrast with Virgil, comes up with hairsplitting subdivisions, makes mistakes,[52] and forces his concepts. The role that Dante attributes to her is perfectly clear from her actions and the epithets attached to her. She is a figuration or incarnation of revelation (*Inf.,* 2, 76): *sola per cui l'umana spezie eccede ogni contento da quel ciel, che ha minor li cerchi sui* ("through whom alone mankind excels all that is contained within the heaven which has the smallest circles"); (*Purg.,* 6, 45): *che lume fia tra il vero e l'intelletto* ("who shall be a light between truth and intellect") which, out of love (*Inf.,* 2, 72), divine grace sends to man for his salvation, and which guides him to the *visio Dei.* Mandonnet forgets to say that she is precisely an incarnation of divine revelation and not revelation pure and simple, although he quotes the pertinent passages from the *Vita Nova* and from St. Thomas, and the above-mentioned invocation, *O Donna di virtù, sola per cui, etc.* One cannot address the "supernatural order" as such, one can only address its incarnate revelation, that part of the divine plan of salvation which precisely is the miracle whereby men are raised above other earthly creatures. Beatrice is incarnation, she is *figura* or *idolo Christi* (her eyes reflect her twofold nature, *Purg.,* 31, 126) and thus she is not exhausted by such explanations; her relation to Dante cannot fully be explained by dogmatic considerations. Our remarks are intended only to show that theological interpretation, while always useful and even indispensable, does not compel us to abandon the historical reality of Beatrice—on the contrary.

With this we close for the present our study of *figura*. Our purpose was to show how on the basis of its semantic development a word may grow into a historical situation and give rise to structures that will be effective for many centuries. The historical situation that drove St. Paul to preach among the Gentiles developed figural interpretation and prepared it for the influence it was to exert in late antiquity and the Middle Ages.

ST. FRANCIS OF ASSISI IN
DANTE'S "COMMEDIA"

ST. FRANCIS OF ASSISI IN DANTE'S "COMMEDIA"

Few passages in the *Paradiso* are as well-known and as generally admired as the eleventh canto; this is not surprising, for its subject is St. Francis of Assisi and the verse is exceptionally beautiful. Yet the admiration for this canto is not entirely self-explanatory. Francis was one of the most impressive figures of the Middle Ages. The whole of the thirteenth century, which covered Dante's youth, was as it were impregnated with his personality. No contemporary habit of life, voice, or behavior have reached us as clearly as his. His character stood out by virtue of its many contrasts. His piety, at once solitary and popular, his character, at once sweet and austere, his appearance, at once humble and striking, have remained unforgettable. Legend, poetry, painting, made him their own, and long after his death, every mendicant friar in the street seemed to carry in himself something of his master, and so to spread it thousandfold. His personality undoubtedly contributed much toward awakening and sharpening the sense of the originality and distinctness of the individual, just that sense whose great monument is Dante's *Commedia*. From the encounter, therefore, of Dante and St. Francis, that is to say, from the entrance of Francis into the *Comedy,* we should expect one of the highlights of concrete life painting in which the *Comedy* is so rich. In the already half legendary biography of Francis, Dante found ample material for the portrayal of such an encounter. It is the more strange that he did not let it take place at all.

Nearly all the characters in the *Comedy* appear in person. Dante finds them in the place God's justice has appointed for them, and there, direct encounter is developed by question and answer. With Francis of Assisi it is otherwise. True, Dante sees him, right at the end of the poem, sitting in his seat in the white rose among the blessed of the New Testament; but he does not speak to him, and in the other passages where he is mentioned, he does not appear himself; not even in the most fundamental, the most detailed of these passages, namely the eleventh canto of the *Paradiso,* where Francis does not speak himself; instead, others give an account of him. However surprising this may be, the form and manner of the account are even more so.

Dante and Beatrice are in the Sun Heaven, surrounded by a caroling band of blessed spirits who interrupt their dancing to make themselves known as Fathers of the Church and philosophers. One of them, St. Thomas Aquinas, names and characterizes himself and his companions, and then they begin the dance again. Dante, however, has not understood the meaning of some of Thomas's words: "I was a lamb of Dominic's flock, where one finds good pasture if one does not stray." For this line—*u' ben s'impingua, se no si va-neggia*—(and also for another passage about Solomon), Dante needs an explanation. Thomas, who, like all the blessed, enjoys direct vision of the eternal light so that nothing of Dante's thought can remain hidden from him, fulfills the unspoken desire for interpretation of his words. Once again song and dance are interrupted so that Thomas, assisted by Bonaventura, can make a commentary on his words. The commentary fills three cantos. In the first of them, the eleventh canto, Thomas tells the life of St. Francis, and adds to it a lament over the decline of his own, the Dominican order; in the twelfth, conversely, the Franciscan Bonaventura recounts Dominic's life and closes with a censure of the Franciscans; the thirteenth canto contains, again from Thomas's mouth, the commentary on the utterance of King Solomon already mentioned. From the two cantos about the mendicant orders, Dante and the reader learn that both orders were founded with the same purpose, that they complement each other, and that in both orders alike the life of the founder was equally perfect and the decadence of the followers equally detestable; that, therefore, in each of them men thrive if they follow the example of the founder and do not stray from it. Both cantos make a didactic commentary, closely built into the framework of Dante's interpretation of history, with sharp polemical passages directed not only against the two orders, but against the papacy and clergy in general. Francis's life also belongs to the commentary. Thus, it is part of a commentary, several hundred lines long, on a subordinate clause which occupies only one line, and which could certainly have been made clear if presented more briefly. The frame, then, is this: Thomas, the great Church teacher, comments copiously on one of his own sayings. Such a procedure is entirely in character with Thomas: but is it suitable for a presentation of the biography of St. Francis? According to our modern way of thinking, no. Through study of the medieval background we have learned to understand the medieval method of commentary. We know that it grew out of the peculiar system of contemporary teaching. We may have discovered also that from the foliage of the epiphytes of commentaries and paraphrases there blossoms sometimes an unlooked-for flower where the supporting tree, that is to say, the text, gives little promise of it; and very often the text is completely hidden by the commentary. Indeed, when we think of many an illuminated initial, of many a liturgical sequence, this phenomenon is not restricted to literature. But here, where Dante is telling the life of St. Francis, could he not have found a less academic, a less scholastic frame?

Furthermore, the biography that Thomas gives contains only a very small part of all the enchanting and overwhelmingly concrete details preserved by the Franciscan legend. The essentials indeed, the birth, the building-up of the work, the death, he tells according to tradition, but he gives nothing of the individual stories to enliven the picture. Even the essentials are given in a documentary way, in chronological order: birth, the vow of poverty, the founding of the order, the ratification by Pope Innocent, the second ratification by Honorius, the journey to the Saracens, the stigmatization, death. Even the wall paintings at Assisi tell much more, and they tell it much more gaily, more anecdotally—not to speak of the other literary treatments of the legend. And there is still something to add: In Dante, besides the outward frame of the commentary of which it is part, the biography has also an inner leitmotiv, and an allegorical one. The life of St. Francis is represented as a marriage with an allegorical female figure, the Lady Poverty. We know of course that this was one of the themes of the Franciscan legend; but was it necessary to make this theme the predominant one? Insofar as we are specialists in medieval art or literature, we have learned gradually and a little laboriously that for certain groups in medieval spirituality, allegory meant something more real than it does for us; in allegory people saw a concrete realization of thought, an enrichment of possibilities of expression.

But this did not prevent one of its most ardent and discerning modern interpreters, Huizinga, from calling it, almost slightly contemptuously, "the rank weeds of the late antique hot-house." In spite of all our knowledge of its meaning, we can no longer spontaneously feel its poetry. And yet Dante, who makes so many people speak directly, gives us the most living figure of the period before his own, Francis of Assisi, wrapped in the drapery of an allegorical account. What almost all later poets have done, what he himself so often did, the art in which he was the first master, that of fashioning people through their own words and gestures in the most concrete and personal way, he has not done here. The Church teacher Thomas recounts the wedding of the Saint with Lady Poverty so that Dante may understand the meaning of the sentence that a man finds good pasture in Dominic's flock if he does not stray.

If we think of the famous allegorical poems of late antiquity and of the Middle Ages, of Claudian's or Prudentius's works, of Alain de Lille or Jean de Meun, there is surely little in common between them and the biography of Francis in the *Comedy*. These works call up whole armies of allegorical figures, describe their persons, their clothes, their dwellings, make them discuss and fight with each other. Paupertas does indeed appear in some of these works, but as a vice or as the companion of a vice. Dante here introduces one single allegorical figure, Poverty, and connects her with a historical, that is to say, a concrete, real personality. This is something entirely different; he draws the allegory into actual life, he connects it closely with historical fact. It is, to be sure, not Dante's dicovery; he inherited it with the whole theme from the Franciscan tradition, where, from the beginning, the wedding with Poverty appears as typical of the Saint's attitude. Very soon after his death a treatise was written with the title

Sacrum Commercium Beati Francisci cum Domina Paupertate,[1] and echoes of the theme are found frequently, for example, in the poems of Jacopone da Todi. But it was not fully worked out; it was scattered in many didactic and isolated anecdotes. The *Sacrum Commercium* contains nothing biographical at all, but is essentially a doctrinal writing, in which Lady Poverty makes a long discourse. Equally, the representation in the Lower Church at Assisi, formerly ascribed to Giotto, shows the wedding as far removed from all concrete biography. Christ unites the Saint and haggard, old, ragged Poverty, while on either side several rows of angel choirs take part in the celebration. It has nothing direct to do with the actual life of the saint; this was the subject of another cycle of pictures. Dante, on the contrary, combines the two; he links the wedding-feast with the impressive, even shrill scene in the market place at Assisi, where Francis openly renounces his patrimony, and gives his father back his clothes. The renunciation of patrimony and clothes, which emerges everywhere else as the intrinsic event of the story, is not explicitly mentioned by Dante; it is woven into the allegorical marriage. Here Francis breaks free from his father for the sake of a woman, a woman nobody wants, whom everyone rejects as if she were death; before all eyes, before the eyes of the bishop, before the eyes of his father, he joins himself to her. Here both the particular and the universal meanings of the incident are at once brought more clearly into prominence than could be revealed through the bare renunciation of particular things. He rejects his father's goods and breaks free from his father not because he wants *not* to possess anything, but because he desires something else and strives to possess that. He does it for the sake of love, for the sake of a desire, which involuntarily wakens memories of other similar occasions when young men have left their families for the sake of evil women who have inflamed their desires. Shamelessly, in the sight of all, Francis casts in his lot with a woman scorned by all, and the reminiscences of bad women become more and more vivid as the theme is elaborated, as we shall see from closer study. It is therefore a strange marriage, repellent according to usual standards, a base union which is here celebrated, bound with strife against his own father, openly, shrilly, and for this very reason more full of significance than the giving back of the clothes, which evokes the contrast between abjectness and sanctity much less than the marriage with a despised woman. And here another memory awakens, of Him who once formerly celebrated another such wedding, of Him who married a despised, abandoned woman, poor rejected humanity, the daughter of Sion. He also, of his free will, gave away his inheritance to follow his love for the abandoned one. The conception that Francis revealed, in his life and destiny, certain correspondences with the life of Christ, the theme of imitation or conformity, has always been fostered lovingly by Franciscan tradition. Bonaventura's biography is dominated by this conception, which also appears in painting, first in the Lower Church of Assisi, where five incidents from the life of Christ are placed opposite five corresponding ones from the life of Francis. The conformity appears also in many particulars, such as the number of disciples, in the community life with them, in the various miracles, and above all, in the stigmatization. Dante did not work the theme out in detail, indeed in general he gives no details; but he consciously worked it into the mystical marriage, thus following it not in isolated occurrences but in the whole and in the fundamentals; although in a way that made it more directly clear to the medieval reader than to the modern.

The biography that Thomas of Aquinas here tells begins with a description of the topography of Assisi. "From this slope," Thomas then continues, "a sun came into the world, shining like the earthly sun when it is rising. Who speaks of this place should call it not Ascesi, but the Orient." This play on words can only serve to emphasize the comparison between Francis's birth and the rising sun; but *sol oriens, oriens ex alto,* is a very widespread medieval conception of Christ himself (following Luke 1:78 and several passages containing the symbol of light in John);[2] this symbol is based on myths much older than Christianity, firmly rooted in the Mediterranean countries, especially in connection with a mystical marriage. For Dante, the birth of the Lord, the marriage of the Lamb, and the vision of Virgil's Fourth Eclogue, which was to him and his contemporaries a prophecy of Christ, were blended with the figure of the Sun-Child as the Saviour of the world for whom the mystical wedding is appointed. There is no doubt therefore that by the comparison with the rising sun, directly followed by the mystical marriage as the first confirmation of the sun-like power of the Saint, Dante wanted to sound the note of conformity to, or imitation of, Christ, and to work it out fully. The metaphor of the rising sun is an exceedingly joyful introduction to which the bitterness of the marriage, ugly and repulsive, stands out in effective contrast. The contrast has already been long prepared-for, and I do not believe by accident. The theme of the mystical marriage has indeed been introduced twice before, briefly, once in a very lovely, once in a solemn and sublime way, both times with all the enchanting beauty of which Dante is capable. The first time it appears as an image, in the simile of the carol of the blessed spirits as a peal of bells ringing to matins, at the end of Canto 10 (ll. 139-46):

Indi come orologio, che ne chiami
  nell' ora che la sposa di Dio surge
  a mattinar lo sposo perchè l'ami,
che l'una parte l'altra tira ed urge,
  tin tin sonando con sì dolce nota,
  che il ben disposto spirto d'amor turge;
così vid'io la gloriosa rota
  moversi . . .

(Then as the horologue, that calleth us, what hour the
spouse of God riseth to sing her matins to her spouse
that he may love her, wherein one part drawing and
thrusting other, giveth a chiming sound of so sweet
note, that the well-ordered spirit with love swelleth;
so did I see the glorious wheel revolve . . .)

(Temple Classics ed., pp. 125 f.)

Here the theme is indicated only by a simile, but it
is made concrete by all its charming joyousness, by its
dolcezza; here as in the following passage, the bridegroom is Christ, and the Church, that is to say, Chris-
tendom, is the bride. In the second place, just before
the beginning of the *Vita Francisci,* it is more dramatic,
more fundamental and more significant: it directly
concerns the marriage on the Cross itself. At the beginning of his commentary speech, Thomas wants to
elucidate for Dante the purpose of Providence. Two
leaders, he says (namely, Francis and Dominic), were
sent by Providence so that the Church could make her
way to Christ with steps more sure and true; and this
"so that" sentence runs (*Par.,* 11, 31-4):

però che andasse ver lo suo diletto
  la sposa di colui, ch'ad alte grida
  disposò lei col sangue benedetto,
in sè sicura ed anco a lui più fida . . .

(In order that the spouse of him, who with loud cries

espoused her with the blessed blood, might go toward
her delight, secure within herself and faithfuller to
him . . .)

(Temple Classics ed., p. 133.)

This is no longer charming, it is solemn and exalted;
the whole history of the world after Christ is, for Dante,
enclosed in the image of the bride who goes to her Beloved. Here also the joyousness, the jubilant passion of
the nuptials is very strong; true, the bitterness of the
agony of that marriage on the Cross is indicated; with
a loud cry, through the holy blood, it is consummated;
but now "It is finished," and the triumph of Christ is
accomplished.

The two passages, one lovely, one solemn-sublime,
both full of nuptial joy, stand as two preannounce-
ments, just as the sun-birth does, in sharp aesthetic contrast with the wedding for which they prepare the way.
Shrilly, with the discord of the struggle against the father, with the hard rhyme-words *guerra* and *morte,*
this celebration begins. And above all, the bride: she
is neither named nor described, but she is such that no
one will open the gates of desire to her—as little as to
death *(la morte).* It seems to me absolutely necessary
to interpret the opening of the gates of desire in the
proper sense as a sexual act, and thus *porta* as the gate-
way to the feminine body. The other explanation preferred by many commentators, that the reference is to
the door of the house, which denies entrance to poverty or death, can indeed be supported by many passages from various texts where it is said that neither to
knocking death nor to knocking poverty will anyone
open the door: it does not, however, fit the bridal context, and it does not sufficiently explain *porta del pia-
cere;* furthermore, Dante would certainly have avoided
such a strongly obtrusive possibility of a sexual expla-

nation if he had not expressly intended it: it corresponds perfectly to the concrete impression of the
bitterly repulsive that he here evokes in general. Thus,
no one likes the woman that Francis has chosen, she is
despised and shunned, for centuries she has waited in
vain for a lover—one of the old commentators, Jacopo
della Lana, explicitly stresses that she has never said no
to anyone—but Francis, the sun rising from Mount
Subasio, openly unites himself to this woman whose
name is still not given, but whose portrayal must
waken in every hearer the image of a harlot, old, contemptible, hideous, but still thirsty for love. From now
on he loves her more from day to day. More than a
thousand years ago she was robbed of her first husband
(Christ, although He is not named), and since then she
has lived scorned and abandoned until Francis appeared. Nothing availed her, neither that she bestowed
peaceful security on her companion, the fisher Ami-
clates (according to Lucan), during a visit, from Caesar; nor that, strong and courageous, she mounted the
cross with Christ, and, as Mary herself, remained at the
foot of it. Now, of course, it is clear who she is, and now
Thomas gives her name: but the sublime and heroic
figure of Paupertas is still not free from a grotesque and
bitter aftertaste. That a woman should climb on the
cross with Christ is in itself rather a stage conception;[3]
still stranger is the application of the allegory to the
winning of the first disciple. However one may interpret the obscure sentence vv. 76-8 syntactically, the
general sense is quite clear: the harmonious community of wedded love between Francesco and Povertà
rouses in others the desire to take part in such happi-
ness; first Bernard (of Quintavalle) took his shoes off
and began "to run after this peace, and while he ran,
he seemed to himself still to be too slow"; then Egidio
and Silvestro took their shoes off and followed the

spouse, the young husband; so much did the bride please them!

To the grotesque and dreadful picture of sexual union with a despised woman, who is called poverty or death and who manifests the meaning of her name in her outward appearance, is here allied an image that, to later aesthetic taste, would be improper to the point of being intolerable: the pious, ecstatic adherence of the first disciples is presented as a love-thirsty pursuit of the wife of another. In the Christian Middle Ages, at the beginning of the fourteenth century, such images were just as telling as they are today, but the form of the impression was different. The corporeal, intense and plastic, found in erotic imagery: to run after a woman, to be sexually united to her, was not felt as improper but as a symbol of fervency. To later taste, of course, the combination of such differing spheres, the mingling of what goes even as far as physical indignity with the highest spiritual dignity, is hard to tolerate, and even today when people tend much more to admire extreme mixtures of style in modern art; yet in a generally honored poet like Dante such passages are seldom understood in their full meaning. For the most part they are neither noticed nor read twice. Of course, it would be even worse to read into them an anarchical extremism as it exists now, and for very serious reasons; Dante is doubtless often "expressionistic" to the highest degree, but this expressionism grows out of a complex heritage; it knows what it wants to express and does so.

The model for a style in which the utmost grandeur is combined with the utmost degradation, according to this world, was the story of Christ, and this brings us back to our text. Francis, the imitator of Christ, now lives with his beloved and his companions, all of them girt with the cord of humility. He is also, like his be-

loved, allergic to outward appearance, and of mean
descent; but this does not make him mean-spirited.
Rather, like a king he reveals his "harsh intention,"
namely the foundation of the mendicant order, to the
Pope; because he is, like Christ, the poorest and the
most despised of the poor, and at the same time a king.
And as in the first part of the *Vita* humility comes more
to the fore, so, in the second part, which deals with the
papal ratification, the journey to the Saracens, his stigmatization and death, his triumph and transfiguration
come out more strongly. Royally he discloses his plan
to the Pope, and obtains the ratification; the band of
friars minor grows, following him whose life could
better be sung in the glory of Heaven; the Holy Ghost
crowns his work through Pope Honorius; and after
he had in vain sought martyrdom among the heathen,
he receives from Christ Himself, in his own country on
the rugged slope between the Tiber and the Arno, the
last seal that confirms his imitation: the stigmata.
When it pleases God to reward him for his humility
with death and eternal blessedness, he commends his
beloved to the true love of his brethren who are his
lawful heirs; and from her bosom, the bosom of Poverty, his glorious soul climbs upward to return to its
kingdom; for the body he wishes no other bier than the
very bosom of Poverty. The whole concludes in a
strong rhythmical, rhetorical surge that leads on to the
denunciation of the later Dominicans; Thomas challenges his listener, Dante, to measure the greatness of
Francis against that of the other leader, Dominic, who
founded the order to which Thomas himself belonged:
Pensa oramai qual fu colui

Beyond doubt Poverty is an allegory. Yet the concrete details of the life of poverty—as elsewhere the
Sacrum Commercium lists them—would not have

evoked so genuine a shudder as the description, briefly but impressively worked out here, of nuptials with an old, hideous, and despised woman. The bitterness, the physically and morally repellent disagreeableness of such a union shows the greatness of the saintly resolution with strong sensuous power; and it shows also the antithetical truth that only love is capable of realizing this resolution. In the *Sacrum Commercium* a feast is celebrated, during which it turns out successively that the brothers possess only half an earthenware vessel to wash their hands with, no cloth to dry them with, only water to wash the bread down with, only wild herbs to eat with the bread, no salt wherewith to salt the bitter herbs, no knife to clean them with or to cut the bread with. One cannot altogether suppress a certain disgust at this enumeration and description; they produce an effect of pedantry, paltriness, and self-consciousess. It is different immediately when one single dramatic act of voluntary poverty is related, such as is often found in the legends of the saints; for example, the scene in Greccio where he sees the brothers through the window, eating at an all too well-decorated table: he borrows the hat and staff of a beggar, goes loudly begging to the door, and, as a poor pilgrim, begs for admission and food; when the astounded brothers, who naturally recognize him, give him the desired plate, he sits with it in the ashes and says: *modo sedeo ut frater minor.* This is a scene that beautifully expresses the peculiar emotional effect of his behavior, but it still does not express the whole meaning of his life. To complete the picture, many similar anecdotes would have been necessary, each contributing a detail to the whole; the biographical and legendary tradition accomplished this, but there was no room for it in the *Commedia*. Moreover, this was not its task. The anecdotes of the legend were known to everyone; more than that, Fran-

cis of Assisi had been, on the whole, a clearly defined
figure for a long time in the consciousness of all his
contemporaries. Otherwise than with many less famous
or more hotly debated characters appearing in the
Commedia, Dante had here a firmly outlined pattern
for his subject, and his task was to present this pattern
so that it stood out in the larger context of Francis's
significance. The reality of the saint's character had to
be sustained not as the specific aim of the presentation,
but as fitting into the order in which that character
was placed by Providence; the personal reality of the
saint had to be subordinated to his office, it had to
shine forth from the office. It was for this reason that
Dante did not describe a meeting in which the saint
could reveal or express himself in an intimate way;
instead he worte a *Vita,* a saint's life. Dante could
scarcely let the founders of both mendicant orders proclaim with their own lips the great significance that
he, Dante, attaches to their efficacy. He presents it
through the two Great Church teachers, Thomas and
Bonaventura, both of them products of the orders. In
both *Vitae* the character is subordinated to the office, or
rather to the mission, to which they were called. With
the cherubically wise Dominic, whose office was teaching and preaching, and whose character could not be
compared with that of the seraphically ardent Francis
in popularity, the individual biography receded even
further, and in its place comes an abundance of images: the bridegroom of faith, the gardener of Christ,
the vine-dresser in the vineyard, the champion of the
sowing of Holy Scripture, the torrent over the fields of
the heretic, the wheel on the Church's war-chariot. All
these are symbols for the office. The *Vita Francisci* is
much nearer to life, but it also is subordinated to the
office; here there is only a single sustained image, that
of the wedding with Poverty, which fixes the form of

the life and at the same time ranges it under the banner of the office. The office is thus the decisive factor
in the biography of Francis also, the realism of the life
must be subordinate, and the allegory of Poverty serves
just this purpose. It combines the saint's mission with
the peculiar atmosphere of his personality, rendering
the latter with the utmost intensity, but always under
the banner of the office; just as Francis himself had
revealed his personality. His strong and passionate
personal realism never wandered at large (*vaneggiava*),
but poured itself into his office. "Franzisce" said God
to the saint in a German Passional,[4] "take the bitter
thing for the sweet, and spurn thyself that thou mayest
acknowledge me." Take the bitter thing for the sweet
. . . Is there indeed anything more bitter than union
with such a woman? But Francis took it, as Dante
shows, for a sweet thing. All bitter things are embraced in this union, all that could be construed as
bitterness and self-contempt is contained in it, together
with love that is stronger than all bitterness, sweet beyond all sweetness, and the avowal of Christ.

Yes, certainly Paupertas is an allegory; but she is not
introduced, much less described, as such; we learn
nothing about her appearance, nothing about her
clothes, as is usual in allegories elsewhere; we do not
even learn her name at first. To begin with, we hear
only that Francis loves a woman in spite of the whole
world, and that he unites himself to her; her appearance comes to us only indirectly, but so impressively
that it is distinct, for all the world shuns her like death,
and, abandoned and despised, she has waited a very
long time for a lover.

She does not speak, either, as Poverty speaks in the
Sacrum Commercium, or as the allegorical figures
Want, Debt, Care, and Distress speak in the last act of
the second part of Goethe's *Faust;* she is only the mute

beloved of the Saint, bound to him much more tightly and truly even than Care to Faust. The didactic strain in the allegory thus penetrates our consciousness not as a didactic lesson but as a real happening. As Francis's wife, Poverty exists in concrete reality; but, because Christ was her first husband, her concrete reality becomes part of the great scheme of world history, of the dogmatic plan. Paupertas links Francis with Christ, she establishes the role of Francis as the *imitator Christi*. Of the three motifs in our text that point toward the imitation—*Sol oriens,* mystical marriage, stigmatization—the second, the mystical marriage, is by so far the most important in this respect, that the two others and Francis's whole attitude are made to develop from it. As the second husband of Poverty he is the successor to or imitator of Christ.

Succession to or imitation of Christ is for all Christians a fixedly pointed goal as it appears from many passages in the New Testament. In the first century of the Church Militant it was shown through the blood testimony of the martyrs that the succession was to be accomplished not morally only in the observance of commandments and in imitation of virtues, but integrally through sufferings like or similar martyrdom. Again and again after this period the integral following of Christ, the imitation of his destiny, was striven for; so that even a hero's death in battle against unbelievers came to be felt as a form of succession. In twelfth century mysticism, apparently chiefly through Bernard of Clairvaux and his Cistercian followers, there developed an ecstatic feeling that sought to achieve an integral imitation of the Saviour through absorption in Christ's suffering, thus in an essentially contemplative way, one in which the inward experience of the Passion, *unio mystica passionalis,* was regarded as the highest stage of the contemplative absorption. So far Francis of Assisi is a continuer of the Cistercian passionate-mysticism, for in his nature also, indeed at its strongest in his nature, the experience of the Passion appears as *ultimo sigillo;* but the path to it is much more active and nearer to life. The succession is based in the first place not on contemplation, but on poverty and humility, on imitation of the poor and humble life of Christ. To the mystical spirituality of the succession, Francis gave a foundation resting directly on Scripture, directly practical and immediately based on life; the imitation of the practical poverty and humility of Christ. This concrete renewal of the integral succession is the reason why Francis was acknowledged by his contemporaries as worthy to receive the stigmata: no one else re-formed the idea of integral succession from the bottom as he did.

Now it becomes clear that Dante could present the reality of the saint's figure in no more simple or immediate way than through the mystical marriage with Poverty, the basis of his *imitatio Christi*. This fitted Francis into the scheme of world history to which, in Dante's view, he belonged: a scheme that in his period was still extremely alive. For the medieval period, and even late into the modern world, a significant occurrence or a significant figure was "significant" in the literary sense; it meant fulfillment of a plan, fulfillment of something foreordained, repeating confirmation of something in the past and prophesying something to come. In an earlier essay on *"figura"* I have tried to show how the so-called typological interpretation of the Old Testament, in which the events are construed as practical prophecies of the fulfillment in the New Testament, particularly the incarnation and the sacrificial death of Christ, created a new system of interpretation of history and actuality which dominated the Middle

Ages and decisively influenced Dante; I must refer the reader to this essay[5] and can here only indicate that the figurative interpretation establishes a relationship between two happenings, both of which are historical, in which each one becomes significant not only in itself but also for the other, and the other in turn emphasizes and completes the first. In the classical examples, the second is always the incarnation of Christ and the happenings connected with it, which led to the liberation and the rebirth of man; and the whole is a synthetic interpretation of the pre-Christian world history in view of the incarnation of Christ. Now the integral imitation with which we are dealing here in the mystical marriage of Francis with Poverty is as it were a recurring figure; it repeats certain characteristic themes of Christ's life, renews them and revivifies them for all to see, and at the same time renews the office of Christ as the good shepherd whom the herd must follow. *Io fui degli agni della santa greggia che Domenico mena per cammino,* says Thomas, and Francis is named as archimandrite. The figure and the imitation together make an image of the completed teleological view of history whose center is the incarnation of Christ; this creates the boundaries between the old and the new covenants; one remembers that the number of the blessed in both covenants, as they are presented in Dante's white rose in the Empyrean, will at the end of all days be exactly the same, and that on the side of the New Covenant, only a few seats were still unoccupied— the end of the world was not far off. But, among the saints of the New Covenant, Francis takes a special place in the white rose, opposite the great patriarchs of old, and just as these were precursors, so he, the stigmatized bridegroom of Poverty, is the most outstanding among the later followers of Christ, appointed to guide the herd along the right way, to support the Bride of Christ that she may hasten to her beloved with sure and true steps.

All these relationships were spontaneously recognizable to the medieval reader, for he lived in them; the presentations of forerunning and after-following repetitions were as familiar to him as the conception of historical development is to a modern reader; men thought of even the appearance of Antichrist as an exact, but delusive repetition of the appearance of Christ. We have lost the spontaneous understanding of this conception of history; we are obliged to reconstruct it through research. But it kindled Dante's inspiration, and we can still feel the glow of it; in spite of our antipathy to allegory, the living reality of the eleventh canto of the *Paradiso* grips us; a living reality that only lives here, in the verse of the poet.

ON THE POLITICAL THEORY
OF PASCAL

ON THE POLITICAL THEORY
OF PASCAL[1]

Fragment 298 of Pascal's *Pensées* is a vigorous attempt
to show the weakness of human justice. It runs as follows in the Brunschvicg edition:

> *Il est juste que ce qui est juste soit suivi: il est nèces-*
> *saire que ce qui est le plus fort soit suivi. La justice*
> *sans la force est impuissante; la force sans la justice*
> *est tyrannique. La justice sans force est contredite,*
> *parce qu'il y a toujours des mèchants; la force sans la*
> *justice est accusée. Il faut donc mettre ensemble la*
> *justice et la force; et pour cela faire que ce qui est*
> *juste soit fort ou que ce qui est fort soit juste.*
>
> *La justice est sujette à dispute, la force est très re-*
> *connaissable et sans dispute. Ainsi on n'a pu donner*
> *la force à la justice, parce que la force a contredit la*
> *justice et a dit que c'était elle qui était juste. Et ainsi,*
> *ne pouvant faire que ce qui est just fût fort, on a fait*
> *que ce qui est fort fût juste.*

A stylistic analysis of the propositions making up
this fragment is not difficult; their structure becomes
immediately apparent if they are arranged as follows:

It is right that what is just should be obeyed:
It is necessary that what is strongest should be obeyed.

Justice without might is helpless:
Might without justice is tyrannical.

Justice without might is challenged, because there are
    always offenders;
Might without justice is impugned.

We must then combine justice and to this end make
what is just strong,
or what is strong just.

Justice is subject to dispute,
Might is easily recognizable and is not disputed.

So
We cannot give might to justice,
because might has challenged justice and has said, it
    is I who am just

and thus
being unable to make what is just strong,
we have made what is strong just.

When the fragment is disposed in this way, it becomes evident that Pascal has developed his thought by
a play of antithetical propositions arranged in symmetrical pairs (isocola). There are six of these. The first
three describe the situation. This situation gives rise
to a problem that can be solved in two different ways:
the fourth pair states the alternative in the form of a
syllogism: it was necessary to do either A or B; A was
impossible; therefore B was done. The second premise
(A was impossible) is strongly emphasized; the reason
why A was impossible is given in the fifth pair of isocola, which is not quite symmetrical since the second
part is longer and more definite. The second premise
appears twice in the final couplet (which closes the syllogism and the whole fragment). The conclusion is presented in two phases: *ainsi* . . . and *et ainsi*. The first

phase (*ainsi . . .*) is a dramatic development of the second premise (note the accent on *elle*); and the second (*et ainsi*), in a tone of bitter satisfaction, supplies the conclusion.

This brief analysis shows a characteristic feature of Pascal's style: its unique fusion of logic, rhetoric, and passion. At first sight he seems merely to be applying a logical method, but the rhetorical clash of concepts in similarly constructed, conflicting propositions introduces a dramatic tension; and when at the end Might emerges from the battle of the concepts, raising its head and lifting up its voice (*et a dit que c'était elle . . .*), its triumph seems to stand before us as a concrete reality.

Effective as this parallelism may be, a critical modern reader, not too familiar with Pascal, may be inclined to suspicion and find an element of sophistry in it. Is not Pascal, he may ask, using the word *juste* in entirely different senses, as if they were identical? In the beginning *juste* signifies genuine, natural, absolute right; but later on, when it falls into the hands of might, it means established, positive right. What is contingent on might is therefore not really right, but only passes as such. But plausible as this may seem to a modern reader, such reasoning does not reflect Pascal's attitude. As we shall soon see, he believed that on this earth might represents not only actual positive right, but legitimate right as well. In order to understand Pascal's thought as he intended it, we must ask how it came into being. For homogeneous and with all its stylistic artifice simple as it may seem to us, it is made up of very diverse influences and experiences.

From Montaigne Pascal derived, sometimes to the letter, the idea that the dominant factor in the laws is not reason or even the natural agreement of all men, but merely custom. But custom is contingent on time and place and is always changing. What is permitted and even praised in one country or period, is regarded as a crime in another; even absurd, arbitrary, and obviously unjust institutions are sanctioned by custom. Nevertheless, custom and the law based on it must be obeyed, not because the law is just but because it is in force, since there is no hope of finding a better one and the disorder involved in any change is a definite evil—which it is not worthwhile foisting on oneself and others, since the new custom would be no better or reasonable than the old one. Pascal took all this from Montaigne, but in taking it over he changed the tone a little, shifted the accents, and ended up with something entirely different. To Montaigne the wavering of custom was no ground for horror or despair; his free, supple, tolerant mind moved courageously, one might almost say comfortably, amid the uncertainties of life; he felt no need of a fixed and absolute order, and I even doubt whether he would have been happy in one. But Pascal did feel the need of such an order and strove for it with a violent passion. He demanded the determinate, the enduring and absolute; he could not abide fluctuations and compromises, which he identified with evil.

Aside from difference in temperament, the change in the times may have contributed to this difference of outlook. Montaigne had lived in a period of political and religious struggles; he had witnessed the clash of untrammeled historical forces; he had seen customs change, and entertained the hope that these transformations and struggles, though he did not approve of them, would result in a stable compromise, which if not good might at least be moderate and tolerable. Pascal, on the other hand, lived in a period of almost complete absolutism, in which one established power, the monarchy, was beginning to wield almost unlimited and clearly arbitrary authority. Still, I believe it was Pascal's character more than the historical circumstances that led him to take a more critical view of custom than Montaigne, to put it down as an evil pure and simple, and gradually replace it by another and entirely different concept: the concept of might. Actually one can read the same idea into Montaigne, for he says that we should obey the law, not because it is just but because it is valid, because it is in force. But according to Montaigne it has force and validity only because it is based on custom. Pascal is inclined to deprive custom of its autonomy, considering it as a function of force, established solely by force. In Pascal we find a problem that Montaigne never treated, the relation between custom and might. Custom without might he calls *grimace;* he finds a decided satisfaction in collecting examples where *grimace* is compelled to cede to might, and in general reducing custom to mere *imagination* or *opinion.* He was not interested in the historical basis of customs, for which Montaigne had conceived a beautiful image—*elles grossissent et s'anoblissent en roulant comme nos fleuves* ("like our rivers, they take on breadth and nobility as they flow")—to Pascal's mind they originated in an arbitrary act of power, the caprice of the legislators. Might could repeat this arbitrary act at any time, radically changing the custom. Montaigne never speaks expressly of might; but it is clear from the general nature of his ideas that for him it could only have been the executant of custom. In his view, two sets of customs, both having force behind them, may perfectly well come into conflict; one may destroy the other; but naked force, unsupported by custom, depending solely on the whim of the powerful, has no place in the *Essais.* Pascal, on the other hand, speaks of the pure power which creates custom and law as it pleases—indeed, as we shall see later on, he says with a kind of bitter triumph that this is as it should be, because there is no other justice than that which is in the hands of might. What, he asks, would become of us, should we try to settle differences according to merit and justice? No solution would be possible. Who takes precedence, you or I? You have four footmen, I have one: the situation is plain, one has only to count.

Here we come to a second set of ideas that helped to mold Pascal's view of justice: the ideas of Port-Royal on the fundamental corruption of human nature. Actually Montaigne also says that we have lost our nature and that only art and custom remain—but he nevertheless puts his faith in human nature, or if you will, in a human nature that history has transformed into custom. He trusted in custom as he trusted in nature, because he was at home in the flow of historical life, and gladly let himself be caught up in it, as the swimmer in water or the drinker in wine. But Pascal accepted the extreme Augustinianism of the "gentlemen of Port-Royal," according to which the world is fundamentally and necessarily evil, in diametric opposition to the kingdom of God; one must decide whether to follow the one or the other.

Here I shall not attempt to discuss the ideas of Port-Royal from a philosophical or historical point of view; this has been done exhaustively in the rich literature of the last century, from Sainte-Beuve to Laporte. Up to Pascal's time, in any case, they did not include a political theory,[2] but at most certain notions about the attitude that a Christian should take toward the world: on the one hand, he should detach himself from the world, on the other, submit to it—the detachment being taken in an inward, the submission in an outward sense. Anyone who can free himself outwardly as well, that is, enter a cloister, should do so. Here as in all things a Christian should follow God's will more than his own, and he is much more likely to ascertain God's will through the circumstances of life than through the essentially unstable movements of his soul. Where a high and responsible social position or family considerations forbid outward retirement from the world, the believer should remain at the post to which God's will has assigned him. Even within the world, you can detach yourself from it by turning your heart away from it, by taking no part in its pleasures and lusts, but participating rather in its cares and sufferings, since suffering is our strongest bond with Christ. As for the submission, it consists in recognizing the institutions, particularly the political and social institutions, of this world, in obeying the secular powers and serving them in accordance with your position; for although the world has succumbed to concupiscence and is therefore evil, a Christian has no right to condemn it, much less oppose it by worldly means, since he himself is in the same state of sin, and the evil of this world is the just punishment and penance that God has appointed to fallen man. The injustice of this world corresponds then to the true justice of God, which we must gladly suffer; where God permits true justice to prevail, he is moved to do so not by justice but by mercy. In rejecting criticism of the world's institutions, this line of thought seems to preclude political theory. Evil as it may be, the world was established by God; a Christian can only submit. Indeed, Port-Royal did not occupy itself with political theory and in all probability Pascal himself would not have done so, if outward events had not brought the political problem home to him.

These events were the incidents in the conflict be-

tween Port-Royal and the Jesuits. If it is a Christian's
duty to submit to the world, it is surely—and far more
so—his duty to obey the Church. The Church is the
community of the faithful, established by God; its
mission is to teach, to administer the sacraments indispensable to all who seek salvation. To stand outside
the Church, to break away from it of their own free
will like the Protestants—for the Jansenists this was
unthinkable. But if corruption prevails within the
Church, if the powers of evil beguile and ensnare the
heads of the Church, the bishops and the pope, and
make willing tools of them; if thereupon the Church,
on the strength of its authority and the obedience imposed on the faithful, constrains the few to whom God
has granted true knowledge to condemn openly and
solemnly what they regard as the very essence of faith;
if moreover the Church, supported by the secular
power and itself acting as a secular power, sets out to
destroy right by might, the consequence will be a situation without issue, a disastrous crisis. Such was the
situation of Port-Royal in the years of Pascal's closest
association with it. He directly experienced most of
this crisis, and inevitably it impressed him as the triumph of evil within the Church itself. In those years
the problem of justice and might became real for him;
this was the period of the *Pensées* and other short
pieces containing his political theory. Now Montaigne's
conception of right as mere custom combined with the
radical Augustinian view of the world as a realm of
evil; the result was the picture described above of custom as an emanation of might, pure caprice of the
Devil.

Pascal was always inclined to carry things to ex-
tremes. In his last years, during the crisis of Port-Royal,
he gave this inclination free rein in the belief, sup-

ported by ecstatic visions and a miracle, that he was doing the will of God. Among the extreme ideas of this period, there are three, closely related to one another, which constitute what I call his political theory: his hatred of human nature (and hence of his own); his condemnation of existing law as purely arbitrary and evil; his belief that this was the only justice which could lay claim to legitimacy.

His hatred of human nature derived from radical Augustinianism. In his famous distinction between *uti* and *frui,* Augustine taught that we should not love the creatures for their own sake, but for the sake of the Creator; that they are entitled to an *amor transitorius* and not an *amor mansorius;* that it is not permissible to love one's own person for itself, so setting it before God, and that this had been Adam's sin. He taught that God is the only enduring object of our love, that all things worthy to be loved are united in Him; that created things are worthy of love only insofar as they reflect His essence. This is a universal Christian doctrine, widely held even before Christianity. In Port-Royal, particularly with Pascal in his last years, it underwent a shift of accent which gave it a peculiar sharpness of radicalism. Toward the end of his life, Pascal is said to have shown those closest to him a certain coldness, to have rebuffed their affection for him on the ground that love among human beings was a theft from God. On a number of occasions he said quite emphatically that love for the creature must inevitably lead to disillusionment and despair. For the object of such love and the qualities for which we love it are transitory. To him this thought was intolerable; he was horrified at the idea that the treasure to which our heart clings should dwindle from moment to moment, that it might be torn away from us irrevocably at any time. For him what is perishable, what must return to nothingness, is nothing: heaven and earth, friends and relatives, our own mind and body; only God is enduring, invariable, immutable; only God is worthy to be loved. Man's frailty and mutability are primarily a consequence of original sin, of Adam's excessive self-love, the grotesque and wicked error which has come down to his posterity and represents what is most hateful in us. Despite his obvious imperfection and mortality, each man invariably regards himself as the center of the universe, loves nothing so much as himself, judges everything on the basis of himself: clearly a hideous error deserving of hatred. And in this connection the word "hatred" takes on a violence of tone peculiar to Pascal.

The word is used in this sense by other Christian authors; it occurs even in the Gospels, in certain fundamental passages in St. Luke and St. John. But I do not believe that this hatred had ever so completely dominated the whole picture of man's love for God. Pascal's famous words about the hateful self are not his most drastic expression of this idea. He said that one should love only God and hate only oneself; that the Christian religion teaches self-hatred; that self-hatred is the true and unique virtue. There are also moderate formulations, but the radical ones set the tone of the *Pensées*. Obviously this self-hatred does not refer to Pascal's fortuitous self, but to the self of every man, since all men share the same transience and the same abominable self-love. Hatred of himself and men was by no means natural to Pascal; he was capable of passionate, even jealous attachments, and he had difficulty in combating a high esteem for his own person, the *orgueil* to which, from an earthly point of view, he was more entitled than most men. His religious radicalism triumphed only by violence over his natural disposition, which itself to be sure contained a good measure of violence. Self-hatred and hatred of mankind, even in the radical form they assumed with Pascal, can be justified by Christian dogma and tradition. But where as in Pascal this motif is emphasized, isolated from other Christian ideas, it threatens to come into direct conflict with Christian ethics. The injunction to "love thy neighbor as thyself," presupposes a love of oneself; without it *one would hate one's neighbor as oneself.* Moreover, such extreme conceptions imply a certain coolness toward creation as a whole; not only man but all created nature is rendered unworthy of our love by its transience. Nature aroused curiosity, admiration, and terror in this great physicist, but no love. Few religious, mystic, or idealistic writers have been further from the thought that divine truth and beauty are reflected in the phenomena of this world. And this no doubt accounts for his emphatic rejection of all attempts to prove the existence of God by the manifestations of nature.

The second idea, the condemnation of earthly law as arbitrary and evil, is closely related to the first, for apart from all experience it follows logically from the corruption of human nature. Our law and our politics —here "politics" is taken in the widest sense, comprising all our dealings in this world—can only be evil, and so they are, as experience confirms. Neither reason nor justice prevails, but chance and violence. Pascal was descended from the *robe,* or bourgeois officialdom; he was a man of the highest intelligence and discernment. Though the most honorable positions were open to him and his class, he was barred from all political freedom, from all activity involving political responsibility. In the epoch of total absolutism the population of all classes had become a mere object and had ceased to be in any respect a subject of politics. His class had just lost the last vestiges of its political independence in the struggles of the Fronde. Still, it seems unlikely that any dissatisfaction arising from these circumstances contributed to his political views. Pascal held aloof from any participation in the Fronde, though involvement would have been quite in keeping with his family traditions. Yet its seems inconceivable that a man of his social and intellectual stature would have held (and acted on) such political opinions at any other time. His certainty that all political institutions are based on delusion, chance, and violence is expressed in his characteristically cutting, paradoxical manner, which sometimes, it seems to me, echoes motives other than Christian. Though intended to support radically Christian conclusions, his critique is open to much broader interpretation. In *Trois Discours sur la condition des grands*,[3] he proves to a *grand seigneur* that his prestige and power are not based on any natural and authentic right, but solely on the will of the legislators—a different whim, a different *tour d'imagination* on their part, and he would be poor and powerless. True, his position, like all existing institutions recognized by positive law, is legitimate; but it brings him only outward deference and obedience (for it is foolish and base to withhold obedience from existing institutions), and no inward respect. Even if according to the standards of this world he uses his power honestly and benevolently—which is his duty— it is always a power opposed to the kingdom of God; for God, who dispenses the goods of love, is the King of Charity; whereas he, who administers and distributes the goods of this world is a king of concupiscence. Even if he governs this kingdom honestly, but does strive to do more, he will be eternally damned, though indeed as a gentleman: *Si vous en demeurez-là, vous ne laisserez pas de vous perdre, mais au moins vous vous perderez en honnête homme.* The kingdom of grace and salvation begins far beyond all human *honnêteté.*

These same ideas recur in the *Pensées,* where the absurdity and fortuitousness of human institutions are described in a way that would be highly revolutionary if not for the Augustinian setting. To give an example, killing is the worst of crimes according to all divine and human law; but if my neighbor, whom I ought to love, lives across the river where another prince rules, and if he happens to be at war with my prince, then I am entitled to kill him, in fact it becomes my duty. He lives on the other side of the river. This is the basis, the only basis of my right to kill him. The whole era of absolutism, the whole era of cabinet wars which the peoples had to endure but otherwise took no part in, is embodied in these words. And it is interesting to observe that such ideas (which were widespread though no one else formulated them so sharply) were perfectly compatible with complete and even hyperbolically expressed loyalty toward the sovereign. Never has an epoch been more nominalistic.

In Pascal, of course, this whole line of thought is based on an extreme development of the idea of the corruption of this world. Through original sin and Christ's sacrifice, the world has become the perpetual murderer of Christ, man has lost his first nature, and any *opinion* or *imagination* can become his second. But what is actually done at any particular time is decided by the right of the stronger, by might. Real power is the only human phenomenon for which Pascal shows a certain amount of respect and esteem, though it is often expressed with an insidious bitterness that seems to border on cynicism. He respects the law of the wicked, precisely because of its candid, unfalsified clarity; and in a number of passages he explains this sentiment in detail. It is not so vain to dress with elegance, he says; it shows that you have many hands working for you: the tailor, the embroiderer, the barber, the valet. What is revealed in this way is not something external, not a delusion, but genuine power; to dress well is to show your power. In their respect for power and its outward signs, the people show a sound instinct though their motives are mistaken: they believe that they must respect might because it is just, and that is a fallacy. Might should be respected not because it is just but for its own sake, because it exists. However, it is dangerous to enlighten the people about this mistake.

Here we approach Pascal's third idea, namely the legitimacy of right based on might. But before going into it I must digress, for my assertion that Pascal respected nothing on earth but power calls for qualification. Actually he recognized another realm, situated between worldly power and divine love: the realm of human thought, of the earthly intellect, which he sometimes (in the second of the *Discours sur la condition des grands* and in fragments 332, 460, and 793 [Brunschvicg] of the *Pensées*) contrasts with the realm of power. He draws careful boundary lines between the three realms; the realm of material power is infinitely remote from the realm of God, and this distance symbolizes the infinitely more infinite distance separating the realm of the human intellect from the supernatural realm of divine charity. The greatness peculiar to each of these three realms is without value or influence in the others: the mighty of this earth, the geniuses, and the saints, have each their own domain, closed to any effective intervention by the others. For Pascal man is a *roseau pensant*, a thinking reed; frailty is his misery, thought his greatness. But this realm of the human mind does not fit in very well with Pascal's political views; how, from the standpoint of practical politics, can we conceive of thought and might as two distinct spheres impervious to each other's influence? Either the human mind can triumph over might or might can repress it. True, Pascal is thinking first and foremost of such relatively unpolitical forms of human thought as mathematics and physics, but experience shows that even these can come into conflict with might, and Pascal himself dealt with one such case, that of Galileo, in the eighteenth letter of his *Provinciales*. It is not sufficient to maintain a theoretical separation between the two realms and to brand any potential infringement of might on mind as an unjustified tyranny that will be unable to repress the truth in the long run, for this would justify revolution in the name of the mind, which is exactly contrary to Pascal's intention. Logically he would have had to abase science and thought to the same level as all other aspects of man; he would have had to put down their activity and achievements as mere opinion and delusion which, like everything else on earth, were dependent, and rightly so, on might. To this he could not consent. That had been easier for Montaigne.

However, where Pascal speaks of political matters, he does not mention the human mind. Thus the inconsistency is not apparent and I can conclude my digression here. In the political world as he represents it, might, that is, evil, rules exclusively—and by right. In elaborating this paradox—the third of the ideas enumerated above—Pascal again goes much further than St. Augustine or his friends of Port-Royal and involves himself much more deeply than the latter in practical, earthly problems.

The moral code of the *honnête homme* prescribed submission to the prevailing political and social powers; to know one's proper place in the existing, established order, and take an attitude fully consonant with it: this was the ethical and aesthetic ideal which was then taking form and which Pascal's friend Méré contributed a good deal to molding. It derived from an old Christian idea which now assumed a new significance: it is the Christian's duty to endure this world and most particularly its injustice, for Christ voluntarily suffered injustice and every Christian should follow in his footsteps.[4] Above all, the Christian should endure political authority, for Christ himself, throughout his life and particularly in the Passion, submitted to the state. Though committing the supreme injustice, this state power which put Christ to death was nonetheless just, for the divine order of salvation prescribed that it should (in conformance with the laws of the state, hence legally) carry out the sacrifice which, as expiation for Adam's sin, was just also in the eyes of God. Christ's sacrifice should be re-enacted in every Christian; all those who are held worthy to suffer injustice, particularly at the hands of the state power, are by that same token held worthy to partake of Christ's sacrifice, and should rejoice. Our joy in the injustice we suffer should be limited only by charity. The only reason why we should not wholeheartedly wish injustice to befall us, is that this would be wishing someone to do us an injustice, and to wish our neighbor to commit an injustice is a grievous sin.

Although this doctrine, to which Port-Royal adhered in theory and still more in practice, relates to injustice in the world, it did not lead to political criticism: it taught men to endure whatever happens in the world, whether it be right or wrong. The question of whether what happens is sometimes or always wrong, or wrong only in particular cases, was not taken into consideration. To be sure Port-Royal followed St. Augustine in regarding the world in general as evil; but it did not ask, and certainly it did not apply the methods and standards of human reason to ascertaining, whether individual legislators and governments might not be moved by God's grace and mercy, so causing a certain amount of justice to prevail, frequently or occasionally, or whether this was never the case.

But on the basis of Montaigne, Méré, and his own experience, Pascal did undertake this inquiry. He combined the negative conclusions of Montaigne and Méré with extreme Augustinianism and thus, in accordance with his temperament, developed the Christian idea we have been discussing into a tragic paradox, both powerful and dangerous.

Through reason and experience Pascal infers that the institutions and the whole process of this world are based on chance and arbitrary power; that our whole earthly order is sheer folly. He believed he was serving the faith by demonstrating, forcefully and convincingly, that misery and injustice, violence and folly, are the foundations of our life; and then he goes on to say that a Christian, fully cognizant of these follies, should obey them, not because he respects folly, but because he respects the will of God who, in order to punish man and open the road of salvation to him while at the same time making it more arduous, has subjected him to these follies; because, accordingly, they are the just law, the only law we deserve. All this, I believe, is dogmatically unassailable; but certain points are overemphasized and (to speak in Christian terms) there is a presumptuous intrusion of rational insights; a faith driven to such extreme of paradox is almost bound to shift into the opposite of faith. In French the word *folie* means both foolishness and madness; thus I am not doing Pascal any great violence, I am exaggerating only slightly if I sum up his thought

as follows: the political order of this world is madness
and violence; a Christian must obey this madness
and should not stir a finger to allay it; for the rule of
madness and violence is God's will, it is the proper justice that we deserve; the triumph of madness and violence, the triumph of evil on earth is God's will. Surely
few men would live under such a paradox and remain
Christians; but Pascal adds, again irrefutably from
the standpoint of dogma but again overstating the
case, that the Christian religion is *la seule religion
contre nature, contre le sens commun*. In the eighteenth century Voltaire and others took Pascal's ideas
as a starting point for rationalistic polemics against
Christianity.[5]

One may incline to conclude from all this that a
Christian adhering to these views—Pascal's or the more
moderate version of Port-Royal—would not be able to
fight for justice and truth. But this is not the case. Pascal himself fought: he is the author of the *Lettres provinciales,* one of the most important polemics in Christian—or for that matter, in all—literature. The
Christian may fight, indeed he must fight as soon as he
is convinced that he is fighting not for his own cause
but for that of God. The Church itself fought in its
beginnings, and even the Church triumphant must
fight against its enemies without and within. But when
can a Christian be sure that he is really fighting for
the truth—when, in this earthly darkness, can he be
certain that the grace of God is with him, that God
has elected him as an instrument of His cause? *Incola
sum in terra,* runs Pascal's favorite Psalm, the 118th,
non abscondas a me mandata tua. In regard to the
signs by which a Christian can ascertain that he is defending the cause of God and the frame of mind in
which he should fight, Pascal has given us a document
which, I believe, should be numbered among the great

texts of Christian ethics. It is part of a letter, first published by Faugère; the date and addressee are unknown
but the letter seems to have been written to a fellow
member of Port-Royal a year before Pascal's death,
during the controversy over the signing of the formu-
lary.[6]

The letter begins with criticism of the behavior of
some of Pascal's companions in struggle. They behave,
he says, as though they were fighting for their own cause
and not for that of God; they seem to forget that it
is the same Providence which has revealed the truth to
some and denied it to others; they seem to believe that
the God they serve is not the God who permits obstacles to stand in the way of the truth; and consequently
they are dissatisfied, grumbling over the difficulties that
beset them and the success of their adversaries. Such
conduct, Pascal declares, is a product of self-will and
self-conceit. For if we ardently desire something on the
strength of our own will, we are angered by obstacles,
because they are something outside us, something neither caused by us nor originating in us, which opposes
us. But if it is really God who is acting through us, we
experience no feelings that do not spring from the
principle of our actions; we face no outside opposition;
for the same God who inspires us permits others to oppose us; then it is not our spirit which combats another
spirit outside us; no, it is one and the same spirit,
namely, God, who produces good and permits evil.
Awareness of this gives peace of soul, and such inner
peace is the best sign that it is really God who is acting
through us. For it is far more certain that God permits
evil, even of the worst kind, than that he wishes to do
good through us, vital as this may seem to us. It is always to be feared that what inspires us is not God but
a secret egoism, and self-examination is far from reli-

able, but often a source of delusion. Far more trust-
worthy than the examination of our inner motives is
the scrutiny of our outward conduct. The patient en-
durance of outward obstacles indicates a harmony in
our soul between Him who inspires our will to fight
and Him who permits opposition to our struggle, and
since there can be no doubt that it is God who permits
the opposition, we may be justified in humbly hoping
that it is He who inspires our will to fight. Some men,
however, act as though their mission were to bring
about the triumph of truth, while in reality our mission is only to fight for it. The desire for victory is only
too human and natural; if this natural desire is concealed beneath the desire to bring about the triumph of
truth, it is easy to take the one for the other and to
suppose that we are fighting for the glory of God
whereas in reality we are striving for our own glory.
Here again our conduct in the face of outward obstacles and the success of our adversary is the most reli-
able test. For provided we desire nothing but God's
will, we must be just as content if the truth succumbs
and remains hidden as if it conquers and is made manifest, for in the latter case it is God's mercy that triumphs and in the former his justice. And Pascal concludes the whole discussion with a reference to St.
Augustine who, commenting on John 17:25 (*Pater
juste, mundus te non cognovit*) declared the concealment of God to be an effect of His justice.

I should like to stress four main points in connection
with this document. First of all, Pascal's distrust of his
own inner movements is highly characteristic and distinguishes him from most other mystics. In his belief,
self-examination is so unreliable, so likely to be falsi-
fied by self-love, that he urgently warns the believer
not to trust in it alone. We have mentioned Pascal's
belief that in deciding whether or not to enter a

cloister, a man should not heed his inner voice alone if important external circumstances oppose the step. Here, in connection with a far more important and universal problem, he refuses to recognize a man's own feeling that he is right and doing good as in itself a valid criterion. Only a perfect peace of mind, based on humility and Christian patience, can prove that the good we think we are championing in our Christian actions really comes from God.

But what is the foundation of Christian patience and humility in such a situation? It is the insight that it is God, and not something extraneous, who permits the obstacles in the path of the good. We are opposed by nothing external, nothing capable of disturbing our peace of mind; God's will alone determines the course of the struggle, and since our will, if we really are fighting for the good, must accord with God's will, our soul must be filled with the peace, the patience, the harmony, which spring from the knowledge that it is the same God who produces good and permits evil.

Here I must caution the reader against a possible misunderstanding: there is nothing relativistic about this attitude, no suggestion of an understanding for the opposing standpoint. Pascal is not saying that "the adversary is right from his point of view," or even that one should try to understand him. He is not interested in the adversary and his cause, but solely in God, whose plan of salvation permits of obstacles in the way of His cause (the obstacles raised by a world that the fall of man has corrupted), so that God's cause on earth seems to be perpetually in a critical, even desperate situation. The few who champion it are by their nature as corrupt as their adversaries; only the grace of God has raised them above the corruption; the possession of grace itself is perpetually endangered and never secure.

A third important point is embodied in the proposition that our mission is to fight, not to win. For this involves the obligation to fight under any circumstances, regardless of the prospects. Such an obligation makes terrible demands, almost beyond the powers of human nature on the combatant. But anyone who succeeds in adopting such an attitude is at least inwardly unconquerable, and even outworldly it will be hard to down him entirely in the long run. Experience shows that ordinary human bravery falters when the struggle seems hopeless—but the man who knows for certain that he must fight regardless of any prospect of success, is immune to despair or panic. And experience also shows that many of the greatest triumphs have been wrested from desperate situations—by men who refused to be defeated inwardly before they had been physically overpowered.

And the fourth, last point: even if, and most particularly if, the truth is defeated and remains hidden, justice is done; for God's justice resides precisely in His concealment of the truth; if He makes it known, it is out of compassion, grace, and love. This is a variant of the idea that we developed above: that to suffer injustice is the justice that befits men. From this it follows that before God no one on earth suffers injustice, or to put it still more sharply, that men can commit, but not suffer, injustice; for although the man who wrongs his neighbor is really doing wrong, the suffering neighbor is one corrupted by original sin, who deserves to suffer. This idea is definitely Christian in its essence and origin; yet the paradox that one can commit but not suffer injustice also has its place in a sphere of thought that is not strictly Christian, provided we interpret original sin as the inextricable fabric of heredity, historical situation, individual temperament, and the consequences of our own actions, in which we are everlastingly involved. Here it will be argued that in actual experience innumerable men suffer injustice every day. Of course it is impossible to prove the contrary; all that can be said is that strictly speaking each man can only decide in his own conscience whether the injustice that has been done him has really been undeserved. If he replies in the negative, this does not excuse, let alone justify, the man who has wronged him, for the transgressor is not authorized to subject his neighbor to an act whose legitimacy he is not competent to judge and the execution of which actually falls to him only by transference. Nor should the defensive position of the sufferer from injustice be weakened by our recognition of the legitimacy of the wrong he has incurred, for insofar as justice is meted out to him, it is by someone other than the transgressor.

The proposition that in the sense described a man can commit injustice but not suffer it, seems to me valuable as an ethical working hypothesis. At least in the initial phase, ethics can only be individual, that is, a question between me and my conscience. Anyone who succeeds in recognizing that whatever happens to him is just, regardless of how wrong others may have been in doing it, has, it seems to me, not only acquired a foundation for ethical thinking and his own ethical attitude, but has also found a new way of looking at everything that happens in the world. But it is no easy matter to make this insight a lasting basis for one's practical behavior.

Let us get back to our fragment. A study of the influences and planes of experience that entered into it was indispensable if we are to appreciate the classical clarity with which the thought is expressed. The expression is based on an opposition between two ideas which are assumed to be universally known and established—whereas the opposition itself shows them to be problematic. Might and justice are contrasted, but at first they are neither explained nor delimited. In the conflict between them, however, their true meaning is gradually brought out, and in the end it becomes clear that they are not opposites at all, but that one is merely a function of the other. When we hear that it is right to obey justice, that justice without might is powerless, that might without justice gives ground for complaint, that there are always wicked men who combat justice, we cannot but assume that Pascal recognizes the existence of an objective justice that is different from might, and at least for purposes of thought, independent of it. But when he goes on to say that justice is always subject to dispute, that might is undisputed and immediately recognizable, that there is no authority able or competent to arrive even at a theoretical decision in regard to a genuine objective justice, and that we are utterly at the mercy of the prevailing justice which is in the hands of might, then it becomes clear that the first premise dealt not with a really existing objective justice but with a mere word, an *imagination*. "It is right to obey justice." Yes, but is there a justice independent of might? Can we recognize it? No, we cannot. Are those who are oppressed by might without justice justified in complaining? Certainly not, for how do we know that they are in the right? Are the transgressors who challenge a justice without might objectively evil? Who can decide? *La justice est sujette à dispute* . . . And what about the might which challenges justice, claiming: I myself am justice. Is it in the wrong? Certainly not. For by what sign can we infallibly recognize justice if it does not predominate? Thus there is no justice other than that which is in the hands of might. Is might then "justice," is it good? Yes, it is justice, but it is not good, it is evil: our world is evil, but it is just that this should be so.

This last thought is not in our fragment, but must be supplied from other statements by Pascal, since it provides the key to the whole. The fragment then consists in a gradual clarification of the relations between the concepts of justice and might.[7] At first they seem to conflict, but one of the two contestants—might—need only show itself, need only stand forth recognizable and indisputable, and justice will renounce its independent existence without a struggle, submit, and become the vassal of might; this is its proper place—with might, not against it.

Our investigation of the influences and planes of experience that produced Pascal's thought enables us not only to understand it more fully but also to appreciate the masterly way in which it is expressed. When an idea is accepted ready-made, because it is current coin, familiar to all—and this has been the lot of many ideas at the end of the nineteenth and the early part of the twentieth century—the expression usually becomes weak and inaccurate because the effort demanded by precise expression is held to be superfluous; an allusion, a catchword, a few familiar phrases suggesting a given trend of thought, seem to suffice; in such cases, a mere word about one of the ideas that are in the air suffices to induce a general understanding or at least a vague feeling of what the author wants to say. But an idea, which, as here in Pascal, is wrested from the writer's own experience by a spontaneous inner activity—such an idea is susceptible of a complete, appropriate expression that precludes the slightest misunderstanding, bars even the slightest displacement or evasion of its exact meaning, and yet permits of an understanding in varying degrees of depth. Sentences come into being which are at once so clear and so profound that a reader who himself aspires to express himself well, cannot withhold a feeling of admiration mingled with a certain envy.

The political ideas of Pascal, which we have outlined here, are in many respects related to those of other contemporary theorists. From the ruins of the political thinking of the Christian Middle Ages there developed two trends of thought, which appear in all sorts of combinations and mixtures. With one of these trends, the doctrine of natural law, Pascal has nothing in common. Nor, it goes without saying, is his thinking in any way related to the older, Catholic form of natural law developed by Thomism, for he did not recognize the idea of a law innate in all men, except perhaps in the Hobbesian form of a natural law that is simply the right of the stronger. But he is very close to the other trend, the empirical statecraft or *raison d'état* of absolutism, generally thought to have originated with Machiavelli. No doubt it had lost some of its spice and freshness since Machiavelli; the free elegance, compounded of Tuscan wit and humanistic boldness, had given way to juridical or pragmatico-political treatises, setting forth systems of politics which were usually methodic but often somewhat fantastic, based on ideas that one may approve or reject, but scarcely love or hate. Pascal's ideas are close to the theorists of *raison d'état,* particularly his contemporary Thomas Hobbes. Hobbes, too, regarded human nature as evil; to curb it, he too demanded a strong state, unimpeded by moral laws, and he demanded absolute obedience to this state, which alone can guarantee peace and prevent revolution. For Hobbes as for Pascal the laws of the state have no juridical basis other than its power; hence we owe them unconditional obedience but no inward faith, just as we owe the state certain sacrifices but no heartfelt devotion. Hobbes's construction is a pure police state, and as has often been noted, this state with all its deployment of force is designed to safeguard the freedom, or better still, the tranquillity of the individual. Pascal comes very close to this, but since in his thinking negative concern for the tranquillity of the individual is replaced by a positive preoccupation with man's immortal soul, the same ideas take on an entirely different coloring. Like Hobbes he stresses the necessity and legitimacy of a powerful state, but he is much more profoundly aware that this "legitimacy" is evil. In Pascal we have not so much a bargain between the state and the individual—in which the individual owes the state obedience and material sacrifices in return for peace and security—as Christian submission to the evil of this world, regardless of whether or not the evil offers the individual any counterpart. In Pascal, too, the purpose or rather the natural function of power is to create and preserve peace—in this connection he cites Luke 11:21; but even if the individual gains nothing by this, even if he suffers perpetual oppression and never gains peace, he must obey. Here Pascal disregards all the theorists of the Renaissance and the Middle Ages and goes back to St. Augustine, whose radicalism he even surpasses. St. Augustine had taught that all government on earth, all power of man over man is a consequence of original sin; without the injustice of the original sin, which had destroyed the natural peace and equality among men, there would be no need for punishment, for the counterinjustice of human power on earth. In the hope of future liberation the Christian must patiently obey this power imposed upon him as a penance: *donec transeat iniquitas, et evacuetur omnis principatus et potestas humana, et sit Deus omnia in omnibus* (*De civitate Dei,* 19, 15, citing Ps. 56:2 and I Cor. 15:24). From this one can infer that the Christian owes obedience to power even when it is evil, but not that earthly power must necessarily be evil. We may conclude (for example, from the chapter on the *paterfamilias*) that in St. Augustine's opinion a Christian state could perfectly well use its power for good earthly ends, although the power of man over man, in itself as an institution, is an evil made necessary by original sin. But Pascal, living in the midst of Christian states, lumped the two orders of evil together. For him power as an institution is an evil deriving from original sin, whence it follows that no exercise of it can be anything but injustice and folly.

In order to arrive at this extreme conclusion, Pascal needed the nominalistic and pessimistic ideas of the theorists of *raison d'état;* he combined them with Augustinianism,[8] so creating a system which despite its appearance of radical Christianity, contained many secular elements and even the germs of a revolutionary social criticism. Nearly all the theorists of *raison d'état* had more or less radically—some approvingly, others disclosing an element of horror—taught that if the state were really to fulfill its ends, it could not adhere to moral laws; fraud and cunning, treason and violence, were permissible; the justice of the state went as far as its might and was based on it. Pascal accepted this much. But the theorists were interested in the state for its own sake; they took it as a value in itself. Like Machiavelli they delighted in its dynamic vitality, or like Hobbes they took a keen interest in the benefit that a properly constructed state can confer on man here and now. All this was totally indifferent to Pascal. For him the inner dynamic of the state did not exist, and if it had existed, he would have regarded it as fundamentally evil. He combined the doctrine of *raison d'état* with Augustinianism and so arrived at the paradox of might as a pure evil, which one must obey unquestioningly, without regard for any possible benefit, but also without devotion, or rather from devotion to God.

"LA COUR ET LA VILLE"

"LA COUR ET LA VILLE"

In seventeenth-century sources two new designations for those to whom literary and above all dramatic works are addressed, take their place side by side with such general terms as *lecteurs, spectateurs, auditeurs, assemblée.* These new terms are *le public* and *la cour et la ville.*

Originally *le public* meant the body politic, the state. Corneille uses it in this sense in *Horace* (line 443: *mais vouloir au public immoler ce qu'on aime* ["but will to immolate what one loves to the public"]) and in *Œdipe* (line 730: *vivez pour le public comme je meurs pour lui* ["live for the public as I die for it"]); it is employed in the same sense by Retz, La Fontaine (*O vous dont le public emporte tous les soins, magistrats, princes et ministres . . .* ["O ye magistrates, princes, and ministers whose very care is for the public . . ."]; *Fables,* XII, 28), and La Bruyère, in whom it is often hard to distinguish between the old and the new sense of the word.[1] Littré's dictionary might lead one to suppose that the new meaning—"an audience" —did not develop until the second half of the seventeenth century; its earliest examples of this usage occur in 1668, in passages from the letters of Madame de Sévigné; but such an inference would be false. Isolated examples may be found in the literature of the preced-

ing century;[2] Racan puts the word into Malherbe's
mouth and it occurs in Théophile;[3] in the sense of a
theater audience it appears in 1629 in the *Requête des
Comédiens de la Troupe Royale:*[4] . . . *depuis qu'il
auroit plû au feu Roy, que Dieu absolve, et à vous,
Sire, les retenir pour leur représenter, et au Public, la
Comédie* . . . (". . . since it pleased the late King,
whom God absolve, and yourself, Sire, to engage them
to play Comedy before you and the public . . ."); this
is the earliest example known to me. Here there might
still be a certain sense of "in public"; but in the
Epître to Corneille's *La Suivante* (1634), the meaning
is quite clear: *Je traite toujours mon sujet le moins mal
qu'il m'est possible, et après avoir corrigé ce qu'on m'y
fait connoître d'inexcusable, je l'abandonne au public"*
("I always treat my subject as passably as I can, and
after correcting what I am told is unpardonable, abandon it to the public"). Here again there is a sense of
"making public," but even more clearly than in the
first example, the reference is to a definite theater
audience that is ready to receive the play.[5] Thus the
sense of "audience" developed little by little, first side
by side with the original meaning derived from *res
publica,* then gradually replacing it. But in itself this
use of the word does not define a sociological group;
its mere occurrence does not imply an educated, well-
to-do audience such as the German *"Publikum"* suggests today. At most it might indicate that the word
peuple was felt to be inadequate. But *peuple* remained
in frequent use for the commoners in the audience. In
itself the word *public* still had little sociological significance; its use in the seventeenth century calls for
analysis and interpretation.[6]

La cour et la ville goes a good deal further in this
respect. As far as I know, it made its first appearance in
the seventeenth century; the earliest examples I have

been able to find date from the 1650's:[7] Boisrobert (in Parfaict, VII, 313) speaks in 1651 of *toute la ville et toute la cour,* Scarron, in 1654, of *la cour et la ville* (Parfaict, VIII, 104); but in the same period we still find such combinations as *le peuple et la cour, le courtisan et le bourgeois, Paris et la cour.* Gradually such words as *peuple* and *bourgeois* became less frequent in this context, giving way to *la cour et la ville;* in Boileau and La Bruyère, for example, this had become the standard term for society and the literary public.

The meaning of *la cour* in this combination is relatively easy to determine; it is the court, the King's entourage. Yet it would not be quite right to identify *la cour* entirely with the aristocracy, although it is sometimes intended in this sense; there were also influential persons at court whose origin and attitudes were those of the grande bourgeoisie; and moreover, as we shall see, the aesthetic attitude of the court was sometimes very much at variance with that of a large part of the aristocracy. It was only very gradually that the court became the repository of literary taste. Vaugelas, who first invokes its authority in literary matters, is still quite cautious. He speaks of "the soundest part of the court," and adds a definition: "When I speak of the court, I have in mind both women and men, and a number of persons in the city where the prince resides, who, by virtue of their communication with the people of the court, partake of its refinement." [8] Here we already see *cour* and *ville* merging into a unity in which neither *cour* nor *ville* is wholly included, but only an elite of each. Later, under Louis XIV, the whole court became a cultural unit. But what of *la ville*? Is it the whole population of Paris, just another word for *le peuple* or *le bourgeois,* or does it refer to the elite that Vaugelas had in mind?

Beyond a doubt it is a particular part of the city

population, and this is what makes it interesting to observe how *la ville* gradually replaced the older terms *peuple* and *bourgeois*—for a knowledge of this process will enable us to interpret the increasing importance of *le public.* The word *ville,* in the sense of an elite—the development is very similar to that of the Latin *urbs, urbanus, urbanitas*—appears in sources older than the formula *la cour et la ville.* When Mathurin Régnier, in his ninth satire, ironically assumes Malherbe's tone, and writes:

> *Belleau ne parle pas comme on parle à la ville*

> (Belleau does not speak as they speak in town)

he actually, as the ensuing references to *peuple* and *crocheteurs à Saint-Jean* ("thieves") show, is referring to the common people of Paris; but here we see how the notion of an urban, urbane elite was able to develop from the spirit of Malherbe, who sought the roots of his work in the popular soil but clipped and pruned his tree considerably. When Corneille, in whose work the locution *la cour et la ville* is still rare, said of himself as a young man:

> *bon galant au théâtre et fort mauvais en ville*

> (a gallant man at theater but a sorry figure in town),[9]

there is no doubt that by *ville* he meant the salons. And by the time the formula became fixed, in Molière, Ménage, Boileau, the meaning of *ville* is evident: it meant Paris society. It might be well to quote a few examples in which the meaning is particularly clear; here is Boileau:

> *Entre nous, verras-tu d'un esprit bien tranquille*
> *Chez ta femme aborder et la cour et la ville?*
> (*Satire* 10, 186)

(Between you and me, would you look on calmly, while the whole town and court came calling on your wife?)

Etudiez la cour et connaissez la ville;
L'une et l'autre est toujours en modèles fertile.
C'est par là que Molière, illustrant ses écrits,
Peut-être de son art eût remporté le prix,
Si moins ami du peuple, en ses doctes peintures
Il n'eût point fait souvent grimacer ses figures.
(*Art poétique,* III, 394)

(Study the court and know the town; both are always full of models. If Molière had thus lent dignity to his works; if less a friend of the people, he had not, in many of his deft portraits, often turned faces to grimaces, he might have carried off the crown of his art.)

Here, moreover, *ville* is contrasted with *peuple;* for Boileau the common people could not be anything but grotesque.

When in Molière's *Le Misanthrope* (I, 1), Alceste, the young aristocrat, says:

la cour et la ville
Ne m'offrent rien qu'objets à m'échauffer la bile

(Neither court nor town offers me anything but things to stir my bile.)

the words simply define his social environment.

And lastly Ménage in Chapter 19 of his *Observations: C'est ainsi que parlent les dames de la cour et de la ville qui parlent le mieux* ("So speak those ladies of town and court who speak best").[10]

Before we go any more deeply into the material and moral structure of *cour* and *ville,* let us examine the relation between the two. Evidently they formed or

came to form a cultural unit. Did each part of this
unit retain its independence, or did the court exert an
intellectual leadership in keeping with its social rank?
Taine takes the latter view when, in his essay on Racine
as a reflection of the manner of his time,[11] he describes
seventeenth-century society as monarchical and aristocratic. Such an inference might seem to be justified by
La Bruyère, but La Bruyère wrote in the 1680's, when
the theater had passed its golden age, and moreover he
is not an easy writer to understand; for he had no systematic purpose and was far from arranging his material as we should like to have it. From his chapter *"De
la ville,"* one may infer what we already know, that the
term referred to a purely social circle, whose main motives of action were vanity and a general desire to im-
press; further, that this society consisted of titled officials *(robe)* and the wealthy bourgeoisie. Here it should
be noted that the two groups were closely related, for
official positions were purchasable and hereditary, and
the bourgeoisie made use of them to better their social
position; we shall speak of this in detail later on. La
Bruyère says nothing about it. He speaks of the foolishness of this class, as reflected in their imitation of
aristocratic manners and the fabulous sums of money
they lavished on their vanity. In a few portraits he
describes their emptiness of heart and estrangement
from both the people and nature. By contrast he even
finds a few kind words for the court; and since in general he regards the follies of the "town" as a caricature
of the court *(Paris, pour ordinaire le singe de la cour)*,
one might in reading him be tempted to accept Taine's
conclusion that the court was the dominant element in
the culture of the seventeenth century, particularly
the second half of it, and that everything else was simply an emanation of the court.

But in the first half of the century this was certainly not the case. The cultural forces at that time did not spring from the court—or from the common people; but from the class that was later to be known as *la ville.* The courts of Henry IV, Louis XIII, and Anne of Austria contributed little to the classical movement that was then taking form, and even Richelieu's patronage and encouragement of cultural life were too erratic and arbitrary to set their stamp on it. Malherbe, Hardy, Balzac, Corneille, and the scholars of Port-Royal were educated and did their work far from the court; their relations with it varied, but none of them was ever decisively influenced by it. *Le Cid* triumphed in spite of Richelieu; the Académie sprang up independently and at first accepted his protection very reluctantly; Mme de Rambouillet and her group, the creators of Preciosity, stayed away from court as a matter of policy. Such men as Descartes, Pascal, and the circle of mathematicians and scientists from which they sprang belonged to the *grande bourgeoisie* (which furnished most of the century's leading minds) and had no close ties with the court. Court influence did not become predominant until after 1660, when Mazarin was dead and Louis XIV had begun to rule in his own right. This was the actual beginning of the "century of Louis XIV," and it did not begin without a struggle. It was in the intellectual conflicts of the first years of Louis XIV's rule that *le public* and *la cour et la ville* finally took form, and in order to understand the nature and composition of the *public,* we must study these conflicts.

The controversy over Molière gives us the clearest idea of them. Molière, who had just registered his first triumphs in Paris, became the protégé, one might almost say the friend, of the King, himself a young man of twenty. The polemics over Molière reflect a struggle between the two generations which cut the century

into two distinct segments. In the first period rationalism, Preciosity, romantic heroism, and *tendresse* lived
side by side and in unstable mixtures; this was an age
shot through with political and religious partisanship.
In the second period all these currents were mastered
and synthetized to form a homogeneous culture.
Through the polemics over Molière in the 1660's, we
can follow the offensive of the new groups and the last
resistance of the old; in his years of struggle in Paris
Molière accordingly tells us a good deal of what we
want to know.

Molière had the court and the "public" on his side
from the very first; he was opposed only by certain isolated groups and cliques, some of which however were
still very powerful. Many of his detractors were merely
envious—actors from other theaters and a few playwrights; various persons who felt themselves to be the
butt of his satire. But as a rule, these personal motives
concealed a more deep-seated hostility. Here we shall
disregard all personal polemics stemming from spite
and envy, and try to make out the fundamental positions.

First there were the salons of the *précieuses*, the *ru-
elles*. Satirized in *Les Précieuses ridicules*, they reappear
in the opening scene of *Les Fâcheux*, and are treated
at length in *La Critique de l'école des femmes*; they
come in for further derision in *L'Impromptu de Ver-
sailles*, where it is remarked that the *marquis ridicule*
had become a stock figure in comedy, taking the place
formely allotted to the *valet bouffon*. The Precious as
we see, were predominantly noble, although a good
many bourgeois aped them out of snobbery. The *"marquis"* in Molière's picture overdo the fashion and
speak a Precious jargon full of fatuous figures and de-
plorable puns; they understand nothing but mouth
their opinions about everything under the sun; mon-

sters of swagger and vanity, they regard themselves as
the lords of the theater, sitting on the stage and im-
peding the performance with their loudmouthed boor-
ishness. They take it on themselves to decide whether
a play is to succeed or not, they regard themselves as
arbiters born, and behave as though the playwrights
were their personal servants. One of them boasts that
half a dozen *beaux-esprits* attend his *lever;* another
that Corneille (the representative poet of the older
generation) reads him everything he has written. On
top of all this, the ladies of the group affect an absurd
demureness. On the whole this criticism is leveled
against Precious society, which was already in full decline. Over against it, Molière advocates naturalness,
common sense, and restraint. This is borne out by his
criticism of the actors at the Hôtel de Bourgogne, especially Montfleury, whose tragic pathos (*faire ronfler
les vers* ["boom out your lines"]) was much admired by
the *marquis*. Molière's satire was particularly inventive
in this sphere, and though it achieved no lasting effect
—the Hôtel de Bourgogne remained the leading theatre—we perceive here an important element of his
general influence. The passage in *L'Impromptu* where
the kings are ridiculed in the style of Montfleury: "You
are not serious? A king must be as big and fat as four
men. . . ." is sure to have aroused a storm of delighted
laughter in the slender, handsome King, who was then
twenty-four years of age; and this scene bears witness
to the feeling of solidarity based on their common
youthfulness, which at that time united Molière, Racine, La Fontaine, and Boileau, a feeling which sometimes enabled Molière to make a kind of accomplice of
the King.[12]

The situation stands out most clearly in *La Critique
de l'école des femmes*. In the debate the comic Marquis
and Lysidas, the pedantic poet, represent Molière's

Precious opponents; Dorante speaks for the author himself. The precious *marquis* are already in the minority, but they have only contempt for their adversaries, the admirers of Molière. But who are these admirers whom the *précieux* despise? First of all, the general public makes its appearance in *La Critique de l'école des femmes* as the *parterre,* the pit.[13] The Marquis of the *Critique* despises the *parterre,* and Dorante, who comes to its defense and speaks for Molière, might seem to be defending the good sense of the common people against the preciosity of the aristocrat; but it is not as simple as all that. For Dorante, who is himself a *chevalier,* makes it clear that he is attacking only a certain part of the nobility; he has in mind only "a handful of gentlemen who dishonor the court by their extravagant manners and lead the people to believe that we are all alike." And we soon have further confirmation of this view. For in reply to Lysidas—the envious pedant who is in league with the Marquis and wishes to annihilate Molière, his successful rival, with the help of the rules—Dorante cites the favorable reception of *L'Ecole des femmes* at court; and it now turns out that Lysidas despises the court just as much as his ally, the Marquis, despises the *parterre*—quite in the style of the older generation of the "precious" Hôtel de Rambouillet, who had been perfectly justified in declining to follow the lead of the crude, uneducated court of their day. But the situation had changed: now the true connoisseurs, scholars, and men of the world were at court; it was here that the best of taste and judgment were to be found—Dorante defended the court against the pedantic Lysidas just as warmly as he defended the *parterre* against the Marquis; in *Les Femmes savantes* (IV, 3), written a few years later, Clitandre speaks to Trissotin in the same terms. Here then is the situation as Molière describes it: *bon sens, naturel,* and *bon goût* are to be met with in the *parterre* as well as at court. The artist must endeavor to please them both; in point of natural, sound judgment the two are allied, though the opinions of the *parterre* are more direct and less subtle than those of the court; the enemies of sound judgment are the precious *marquis* and extravagant pedants, who look down on the court as well as the *parterre.* Boileau gives us a similar impression, except that he substitutes Paris society, *la ville,* for the *parterre.* We shall come back to this question of the character and composition of the *parterre,* for it may lead us to revise in no small measure the tentative picture of the theater public derived from our analysis of *la cour et la ville.* Suffice it to say here that the cultural unity which made its appearance in the 1660's and which provided the foundation of the great classical age, resulted from an alliance, if not an inner kinship, between the King and his entourage, on the one hand, and certain strata of the urban population, whose sociological position remains to be defined, on the other; that this alliance was directed against preciosity and pedantry; that the common battle cry, whether justified or not, was *bon sens* and *naturel.* Beyond any doubt, the King and the court were the conspicuous representatives, the social leaders of this alliance; but this does not tell us who provided the substance of the new attitudes: it does not clarify their social origin. In any event, we shall be able to identify them with the court aristocracy only if we bear in mind that this class had undergone great changes since the preceding century. But even so, the court had more to do with developing than with originating the new ideas. The King adopted them because they fell in with the original sound health and exuberance of his spirit and with his quite unaristocratic policies. By virtue of his extraordinary power they underwent a change; at first their patron and protector, he became their center and goal. But in origin they remained, not exactly popular, but bourgeois, essentially a vindication of good sense and natural ways against aristocratic affectation. What makes it so difficult to appraise the situation is that both parties to the conflict expressed themselves in a late baroque style which as a whole strikes us as mannered and courtly. And yet what is expressed in the formula *la cour et la ville* is a real alliance, a harking back to Malherbe against Vaugelas and the *précieux*. It is characteristic, for example, that the same anecdote should have been related both of Malherbe and Molière:[14] both were said to have read their writings to servants or children to test their effect. At the same time the formula is a recollection, on the aesthetic plane, of the old alliance between King and bourgeoisie, which had forged the unity of France. From this alliance, as we shall show in detail—the actual "people" were radically excluded.

Another group of Molière's adversaries appears in *Tartuffe;* this is the *cable des dévots,* again a clique, but far more powerful and self-assured than the Precious remnant. Molière triumphed over them only with great difficulty; if he succeeded, it was only because the King's humor and "popular" common sense far outweighed his insight into the bitter spiritual reality of the time. For the play actually undermined the only form of Christianity which was then possible. Those who, like Tartuffe's adversaries, succumbed to natural ways, were lost as Christians. They were cast into a world that had ceased to be Christian; for it was no longer a world of sinning Christians, but a non-Christian world. When once in the course of the long struggle Molière called on Monsieur de Lamoignon, president of the Parlement of Paris, who as representative of the absent King had prohibited the performance

of *Tartuffe* (the King had approved it before his departure), the president said to him: "I am convinced
that it (your comedy) is very fine and instructive; but
it is not the concern of comedians to instruct men in
matters of Christian morality and religion; it is no
business of the theater to preach the gospel." [15] The
sentence is remarkable for its pious arrogance, hypo-
critical politeness, and self-assurance. But it would
have been impossible in a Christian world. Two hundred years earlier no one would have contested the
theater's right to preach the gospel and Christian morality. But Molière was confused and found no answer.
He framed a reply only some years later in the preface
to the printed edition of *Tartuffe;* but by then it had
lost its relevance; and moreover Molière was not justified in giving it. For he did not preach Christianity in
his theater, and his audience expected nothing of the
kind from him.

Yet with the King's help Molière triumphed over
the *dévots.* But powerful as this group was and important as were the problems surrounding it, it is not
properly pertinent to the present study, for—as a group
at least—it did not form part of the theater audience.
Here it is mentioned only because the controversy over
Tartuffe throws light on the attitude of the King and
the actual *public.* When the King finally sanctioned
public performances of *Tartuffe* over the opposition
of the *dévots,* he was not pursuing the principles of a
monarchic cultural policy, but acceding to the spirit
of the Paris theater audience.[16] Political considerations
led him to hesitate, to wait for a favorable moment;
when such a moment presented itself after the *paix de
l'église* of 1669, he followed his natural bent and
obliged the Parisians, Molière, and himself by author-
izing public performance of the play: to the Parisians
he gave the pleasure that he himself had derived from

Tartuffe; to Molière he granted the success and ample receipts; and to himself the satisfaction of putting one over on the *dévots,* who were always trying to interfere with his pleasures—including those of another and more personal kind. To be sure, the monarchy made its own use of the spirit of *bon sens* with which the play is imbued; but in its nature and origin this was far from being an authoritarian, monarchical spirit; it was the spirit of the emancipated middle class. A few decades later, in the days of Madame de Maintenon, Louis would have acted very differently. By then, he had become a pure authoritarian monarch, even in his cultural policy. But in the early years of his reign— and those were the great days of Molière, La Fontaine, Boileau, and Racine—he felt and acted in the spirit of the Paris public, in opposition to the precious, pious, and in large part aristocratic circles which were trying to resist the new spirit of court and city.

Thus the spirit of the great classical age was not simply fashioned by the court and the aristocracy; nor was it by any means what we should call popular— this much we have learned from our analysis of *la cour et la ville.* But we were speaking a moment ago of the *parterre,* to whose judgment Molière attaches so much importance—what is the relation of *parterre* to *ville;* and does the term refer to the common people? It would almost seem to, for in the above-mentioned passage in *La Critique de l'école des femmes,* Dorante, the spokesman of the *parterre,* declares "that good sense has no set place in the house; that the difference between a demi louis d'or and fifteen sous has no bearing whatever on good taste; that, standing or seated, one can express poor judgment; and that, generally speaking, I should set considerable store by the approval of the *parterre,* for among those who compose it, there are quite a few persons capable of judging a play by the rules, while the rest judge in the right way, which is to let yourself be captivated, to eschew blind opposition, affected approval, or exaggerated delicacy." This would suggest that the *parterre* was occupied by the "uneducated common folk" and a sprinkling of impoverished connoisseurs. In order to clarify its position and significance, we shall have to look a little more deeply into the available sources.

The *parterre* was by far the cheapest part of the theater; it consisted entirely of standing room; for ordinary performances the places cost 15 sous,[17] as we learn not only from *La Critique de l'école des femmes,* but also from some well-known lines in Boileau's ninth satire, which also tell us something about its habitués:

> *Un clerc, pour quinze sous, sans craindre la holà,*
> *Peut aller au parterre attaquer Attila.*

> (A clerk, for fifteen sous, without fear of interference, can attack Attila in the parterre.)

Here the young clerks from the courts of justice and administrative offices are represented as the typical members of the *parterre* audience. In his dictionary, which appeared at the end of the century Furetière writes: *"Parterre* also means the floor of a playhouse, where the people stand," and he adds: "It would be the best place in which to attend a play if not for the troublemakers that are to be found there and the quarrels that occur."

Both these testimonies indicate that the *parterre* must have been a rather turbulent spot, and this is confirmed by all the other seventeenth-century reports that I have been able to find. At the end of the sixteenth, and deep into the seventeenth century, the Hôtel de Bourgogne was a place of doubtful repute, in which no respectable citizen, and above all no woman of the better classes, would set foot.[18] A prologue pub-

lished in 1610 by the burlesque comedian Bruscambille gives us an idea of the treatment to which the
audience was subjected and of the general atmosphere
in the theaters of this early period.[19] In his *Prologue
sur l'impatience des spectateurs,* he writes:

> . . . no sooner have you entered this place of enter-
> tainment than, on the very threshold, you shout with
> all your might: begin, begin . . . now really—we have
> had the patience to wait for you without faltering, to
> take your money at the door at least as willingly as
> you have tendered it. . . . But it is far worse after the
> play has begun: one coughs, another spits; one farts,
> another laughs; one scratches his arse; why, the very
> pages and lackeys have turned up; sometimes exchang-
> ing blows, sometimes raining stones on those who are
> unable to reply. . . . As for this class of people, I
> consign them to their masters who, on their return, no
> doubt, will apply a poultice of stirrup leather to their
> hind parts and quell the ardor of their insolence.
> . . . It might be well in passing to administer a cor-
> rection to certain peripatetics who stroll round during
> the performance, which is just as absurd as singing in
> bed or whistling at the table. All things have their
> time, every action should conform to one's reason for
> undertaking it. The bed for sleeping, the table for
> drinking, the Hôtel de Bourgogne for hearing and
> seeing, seated or standing, as motionless as a newly
> wedded bride. . . .

Clearly Bruscambille's audience included a strong
element of what we call the city mob. Through the influence of Alexandre Hardy and his immediate suc-
cessors, this state of affairs was gradually remedied.
But the process was very gradual and the *parterre* was
hard to educate. When a theater moved into their
neighborhood in 1633, the residents of the rues Michel-

le-Comte and Grenier-Saint-Lazare succeeded in having it closed down—their petition referred to the obstruction of traffic in the narrow streets "inhabited by several persons of quality and officers of sovereign courts," and complained of the robberies and acts of violence that resulted from the presence of such an establishment.[20] This attitude was modified in the course of time, thanks largely to Corneille—whose *Polyeucte* was particularly influential in this respect—and to the patronage of Richelieu, who took measures to rehabilitate the theater and raise its tone. A decree of 1641 forbade the comedians, who already included such well-known artists as Mondory and Bellerose, to make use of obscene objects and words, and at the same time gave them full civil rights.[21] This was the first of a long series of ordinances extending over the whole century, whose main purpose was to educate the public. The authorities were compelled to take repeated measures against the turbulent *parterre,* against the pages and lackeys, the uproarious soldiers, the nondescript rabble. We find numerous accounts of brawls and uproar in the theaters, of individuals and groups crashing the gate, of wounded and slain gatekeepers. Parfaict even speaks of an author who boasted that four gatekeepers had been killed at the opening of his play—could one conceive of a greater success? [22] It is true that Chappuzeau, in 1674, writes as though all this were a thing of the past:

> The gatekeepers . . . in the same number as the ushers and at the same doors, are commissioned to prevent possible disorders and, to this end, before the King's order strictly prohibiting admission without payment, the individual chosen was a stalwart who also knew how to distinguish reputable people from those of different mien. They stop those who try to pass without a ticket. . . . The Hôtel de Bourgogne no longer

uses them, except at the main gate, and by virtue of the King's declaration, they take as many soldiers as necessary from his Guards regiment; and the other troupe,[23] which has gatekeepers, can do the same when necessary. In this way all disorders have been banished, and the bourgeois can visit the Comedy with pleasure.[24]

But the King's decree to which Chappuzeau refers[25] had been issued only a short while before, and his account shows how necessary the measure was; moreover, as can be seen from the above-cited passage from Furetière[26] and similar late sources, it brought no lasting results. As late as 1687, the players of the Comédie Française (founded in 1680) were expelled from their theater and had the greatest difficulty in finding a new one. In every suitable quarter they met with protests on the part of the population and particularly the clergy.[27]

Yet Chappuzeau's account shows that the *parterre* also included another class of the population, which required protection against the unruly rabble— namely, the bourgeoisie. The old audience of lackeys, soldiers, pages, young *clercs,* and nondescripts, always inclined to tumult, were gradually crowded out by the middle bourgeoisie. They never disappeared entirely and still provide the atmosphere of the French theaters with a kind of seasoning; as long as they remain within certain limits, they often meet with the sympathy and amused approval of the high-spirited bourgeois (the *malin*). But from then on the bourgeoisie became the predominant element in the *parterre,* which was also frequented by the writers and critics, or at least by those who had not achieved too much prominence. It is unquestionably this largely bourgeois audience of the *parterre,* with its sprinkling of literary men, on whose judgment Dorante—and with him Molière—

relies. But he was not the first to express this point of
view. The *parterre* is lauded in very much the same
way in a book by Charles Sorel which appeared in
1642, at the height of Corneille's success:[28] true, it is
often a noisome place with its "swarm of a thousand
rogues mixed in among the respectable people," and
the hubbub they make; but even so, don't let that
deter you from frequenting the *parterre,* for it is the
best part of the house in which to hear and see, better
than most of the loges; and no need to turn up your
nose, for "sometimes you will find highly reputable
persons there, and actually most of our poets, who
are the persons best able to judge plays, are never
found elsewhere." Twenty years later, such favorable
judgments are frequent. A defender of Molière's *Le
Cocu imaginaire (Sganarelle),* which had been violently attacked, declares that Molière's comedies were
excellent, "for not only has the court approved them,
but also the people, who in Paris are perfectly capable
of judging this variety of work"—and goes on to say
that the success of *Sganarelle* was all the more estima-
ble in that the play had been presented in the summer
and during the celebration of the King's wedding,
when nearly all the "people of quality" had been absent from Paris: "and nevertheless there were enough
persons of quality to fill the loges and the theater of
the Petit-Bourbon forty times over, and enough bourgeois to fill the *parterre* as many times."[29] Here, as in
many documents of this time, the *parterre* is definitely
identified with the bourgeoisie, and no distinction is
made between *bourgeois* and *peuple;* both are contrasted with the *personnes de qualité.* We find no evidence that the taste of the bourgeois differed consist-
ently and fundamentally from that of the noble spec-
tators; I am inclined to think that it did not. In the
course of the 1640's several witnesses remark that the

bourgeois found it hard to get used to the "classical" tragedy and its rules, that he preferred changes of scene, romantic adventures, elaborate sets. But the same was true of many nobles. A little later, the fashion turned to mechanical contrivances, *pièces à machines*. In his *Muse historique* of 1661, Loret speaks of the "changes of scene, beloved of the bourgeois"; but the tastes of the court were no different. And concerning the bourgeoisie La Fontaine wrote:

> *Des machines d'abord le surprenant spectacle*
> *Eblouit le bourgeois et fit crier miracle;*
> *Mais la seconde fois il ne s'y pressa plus,*
> *Il aima mieux le Cid, Horace, Héraclius.*[30]

(At first the amazing spectacle of the machines dazzled the bourgeois, who cried out as though he had beheld a miracle. But the second time he stayed away, preferring *Le Cid, Horace, Héraclius.*)

If we also take account of the King's growing enthusiasm for ballets, operas, and pageants, we are bound to conclude that there was no fundamental difference between the taste of the bourgeoisie and of the aristocracy. In any event it cannot be maintained that the bourgeois preferred the lower genres and was repelled by the noble style. Corneille and Racine enjoyed the admiration of the bourgeois. When in 1660 the Hôtel de Bourgogne gave a free performance to celebrate the peace of Saint-Jean-de-Luz the play chosen was a classical tragedy, Thomas Corneille's *Stilicon,* which is described as *contribuant de bonne grâce, au plaisir de la populace.*[31]

But what exactly was a bourgeois in seventeenth-century France? We find a few representatives of this class in Molière's comedies. Gorgibus in *Les Précieuses ridicules,* Monsieur Jourdain in *Le Bourgeois Gentil-*

homme, Chrysale in *Les Femmes savantes,* are bourgeois; the families in *L'Avare* and *Le Malade imaginaire* are bourgeois. All are members of prosperous
old-established bourgeois houses. But we learn very
little about their actual economic foundations—of
which we shall have more to say below—nor do we
know whether to regard them as typical theatergoers.
We do, however, have ample evidence pointing to a
definite group of Parisian burghers as characteristic,
almost proverbial denizens of the *parterre:* these are
the *marchands de la rue Saint-Denis.* According to an
anecdote recorded by Marmontel,[32] even so early a
dramatist as Corneille hoped for a *parterre composé
de marchands de la rue Saint-Denis."* For a later period
there are innumerable records. In 1662, for example,
D'Aubignac wrote a polemic in answer to the younger
Corneille, who had suggested that before criticizing
his *Persée et Démétrius* detractors should first write
better plays themselves. "Would he," wrote D'Aubignac, "wish to leave his reputation in suspense until
all the *marchands de la rue Saint-Denis* have had time
to write better comedies than his?" [33] And Visé's *Zélinde,* a comedy attacking *L'Ecole des femmes,* takes
place in the house of a "lace merchant of the rue
Saint-Denis," who turns out to be a regular occupant
of the *parterre;* he speaks of "fifteen or sixteen merchants in this street who . . . for the last thirty
years . . . have attended all the comedies that have
been played; and . . . all the most illustrious bourgeois in Paris cite the opinions of these gentlemen." [34]
Most interesting perhaps is a passage in Boursault, in
which he speaks of the first performance of Racine's
Britannicus (1669) and reports that the *parterre* had
not been as crowded as he had feared. Luckily another
theatrical event "had attracted all those merchants of
the rue Saint-Denis who go regularly to the Hôtel de

Bourgogne for the first showing of all the works presented there; in consequence I was quite comfortable. . . ." [35] Here again the merchants of the rue Saint-Denis are shown to be regular devotees of the *parterre*.

It does not seem too rash to think of this proverbial occupant of the *parterre* as typical. Were these theatergoers the "people"? Not in the Christian medieval sense, nor in either of the modern acceptances of the word: they were neither the "proletariat" nor the "nation." They were not the "bourgeoisie" or even the "petite bourgeoisie" of Marxian class struggle,[36] but merely a small and clearly circumscribed group, namely the shopkeepers, the *boutiquiers,* and more specifically dealers in articles of luxury and fashion. In the seventeenth century, the *quartier Saint-Denis* was approximately what the rue de la Paix is today, or at least what it was until very recently. It was the quarter of the tailors, glovers, lace dealers, jewelers; here also were the most celebrated dealers in optical instruments, musical instruments, fine glassware; it could boast the presence of a *fabricant de mouches,* and of maître Jean Bourgeois, *épinglier de Sa Majesté la Reine.*[37] Here then was a section of the grande bourgeoisie, depending for their prosperity on the consumers of luxury articles, that is, on "society." They belonged to the class which lamented the departure of the court during the Fronde and helped appreciably to paralyze the city's power of resistance. They enjoyed a considerable influence. When the omnibuses suggested by Pascal were introduced in Paris, they were the first to demand a line running through their quarter.[38] Despite their wealth these merchants seldom went to the expense of a loge—and then, as we learn from *Zélinde,* chiefly to shield their womenfolk from the crowding, the hubbub, and the undesirable neighbors. They themselves preferred the *parterre.* You had a good view of the stage, and it was cheap.[39] In this they were motivated by bourgeois thrift and no doubt by a certain (equally bourgeois) diffidence. The open and unvarnished domination of the successful businessman did not set in until much later; the best loges, not to mention the places on the stage, were still regarded as a prerogative of the aristocracy and the upper *robe*.

What does this investigation of the *parterre* tell us? It tells us that the *parterre did not represent* "the people," not at least in the sense in which we have come to use the word, but a class eminently suited to merge its inner life with that of the court, to follow its lead, and out of snobbery and ambition, to adopt its attitudes. And so far we have not even considered the connecting link, the widely ramified class of officials *(robe)*, the lower and middle ranks of which belonged to the *parterre,* while the higher grades were numbered among the *gens de condition.* Merely from our study of the *bonne bourgeoisie,* the higher class of tradespeople, we have seen that sociologically the *parterre* was an appendage to court society, that *la cour et la ville* formed an integral unit. The bourgeois in the *parterre* had only a negative and formal sense of his own class—he knew his limitations, the social barriers confronting him—*il se connaît,* as they said at the time. But he was of one mind with court society, and this is what made possible the remarkable unity of style and taste that characterized the great century. Here we seem to be falling back upon Taine's thesis that the court was the truly dominant force in classical French culture. But in the following it will be made clear that this is not our opinion. We believe, rather, that the dominant spirit sprang spontaneously from both classes and cannot be identified with either. But first we must adduce internal evidence of what we have tried to show in sociological terms, namely that the *parterre* was far removed from the common people and represented no independent class.

If the *parterre* had been the common people, it would have rejected the subject matter of the classical theater. For it gave the common man nothing that was in any way related to his life: it reflected neither his daily concerns, nor a living myth, nor the history of his country.[40] Popular types appear in some of the comedies, but in burlesque roles clearly intended to amuse their social superiors; they were never portrayed seriously. The more refined of the comedies and all tragedy dealt with matters that had no meaning for the common people. They presupposed in their audience a state of mind which was beginning to be relatively widespread, but only among the upper classes—today we should call it "cultivated" or "cultured." Critical opinion was formed by this "culture" and we have no evidence that the *parterre* ever rebelled against it. There was no special word for "cultured"; such words as *poli, galant, bel-esprit, honnête,* come close to it from different angles, but never quite hit the mark. Often the notion was expressed by the word *savant,* implying that knowledge is the foundation of good taste. But this knowledge was not limited to scholars; actually erudition seemed, as often as not, to stand in its way—as we can see from *Les Femmes savantes,* particularly the dialogue between Clitandre and Trissotin (IV, 3). In *Le Misanthrope* (III, 1) Molière makes fun of the Marquis, who could do everything without having learned anything, who expressed opinions about all sorts of matters that he had never seriously looked into:

> *Pour de l'esprit, j'en ai, sans doute, et du bon goût*
> *A juger sans étude et raisonner de tout;*
> *A faire aux nouveautés, dont je suis idolâtre,*
> *Figure de savant sur les bancs du théâtre. . . .*

(Indeed I have plenty of wit and good taste; I can judge without study and talk about everything; and on the benches of the theater I can put on a show of learning about the novelties I am so fond of. . . .)

Yet fundamentally the *marquis* were right. The requisite judgment was conferred by the spirit of the century, which also embraced the necessary knowledge. Spirit and knowledge in one were inculcated at the Jesuit schools, by the tutors and preceptors, and above all by social relations. Certain notions of classical mythology and history, which might have passed for learned in the sixteenth century, had by the seventeenth become the common property of all polite society. Thanks to the "purifiers" from Malherbe to Vaugelas and to the salons of the *précieuses,* the correct use of the language had become the apanage of all good society—the scholars of language were themselves bent on establishing *le bon usage,* again a prerogative of polite society. Since the turn of the century, moreover, the criteria by which to judge a work of art, the action and characters of a play, the sentiments and ideas expressed in it, had spread from a small group of learned men to all cultivated society. This had been accomplished by translations and paraphrases of the most important critical texts of antiquity and concomitantly by the works of art themselves as well as the public discussions among literary men and connoisseurs, in the course of which the learned rules of humanistic aesthetics were adapted to the needs of cultivated society. The conflict between popular spontaneity and the learned principles of art, still widely prevalent in the sixteenth century, vanished; both disappeared almost entirely, replaced by an almost solid front of cultured public opinion. Even the conflicts within it, violent as they often were, rested on a common foundation which excluded the "uncultured."

The result was a cultured aesthetic criticism; one need only consider its most significant and most generally accepted catchwords, *vraisemblance* and *bienséance,* to recognize how far removed it was from "the people."

Vraisemblance, on which the new argument for the "unities" was essentially based, marks a way of thinking which found change of scene improbable and therefore objectionable because the stage was small and could never be anything but the same stage, and rejected extension of time because of the brevity of the performance. This notion of *vraisemblance* is typical of cultivated society. It combines the arrogant rationalism that refuses to be taken in by imaginative illusion with contempt for the *indocte et stupide vulgaire* which is perfectly willing to be taken in. The third unity, rational unity of action, brings up a more fundamental problem. There was no need to think of it in connection with the serious medieval drama, because it was there to begin with. Unity was embodied in the history of the world and salvation from Adam to Jesus and the last Judgment. It was always present in the mind of the spectator and moreover it was constantly brought home to him by the arrangement of the stage. Every place, every time, every object, every level of style, fit into this all-encompassing frame. Only when the frame was lost, when there had ceased to be a Christian people and a homogeneous Christian view of the world, did it become necessary to worry about unity. The medieval drama and all medieval art could treat of anything they pleased with great freedom. Within the frame there were no barriers; time and place could change at will; all sorts of happenings could take place side by side thanks to their common frame of reference. And above all, no one objected to the lowly comedy of everyday life in the midst of solemn tragedy. Everything had its relation to the whole and its necessary place within it. And this brings us to the second criterion, *bienséance.*

The notion of *bienséance* comprises a mixture of ethical and aesthetic considerations, cemented by a subtly developed sense of tact. In it morality, rules of social conduct, and aesthetic measure are scarcely distinguishable. Practical morality, the morality that deals in ethical and inethical behavior, is in any case the weakest element in *bienséance,* while the strongest is a purely social prudery, largely in regard to vocabulary. This we discern in *La Critique de l'école des femmes,* and in a more serious vein in a few memorable words of Corneille. The failure of his *Théodore* was attributed in part to the menace of prostitution hanging over Theodora. "In this catastrophe," wrote Corneille in his *Examen,*[41] "I can only congratulate our stage for its purity, when I observe that a tale, which is the fairest ornament of the second book of St. Ambrose, is too licentious to be tolerated on it. What would they have said if, like the great doctor of the Church, I had exhibited the maiden in that infamous place. . . ."

This moral aspect of criticism never had much success where an important work was concerned, for it had the cult of the passions to contend with. The critics who tried to outlaw Chimène's love or Phèdre's declaration to Hippolyte on grounds of *bienséance* were soon reduced to silence. Far more influential as a criterion of criticism was another component of *bienséance,* the appropriate. A king was frowned upon for not behaving royally enough, a princess for being too intimate with her intimates, and so on; this was carried to absurd lengths, as for example when it was argued that since Oreste, in *Andromaque,* was a king's son, it was inappropriate for him to appear as a mere envoy. But the most important exigency of *bienséance* was that no physical indication of human frailty and mortality must be shown in the tragic theater; only in comedy, as comic elements and within the limits of decency, could such things be tolerated. The death of Phèdre on the stage—she appears already dying in order to deliver her confession—was very close to the limit of the acceptable. Under no circumstances might a tragic hero appear physically reduced, old, sick, frail —this theater had no Lear nor Oedipus; if such characters appeared, they had to be remodeled in accordance with the dictates of *bienséance*. The separation of the genres was carried much further than in the ancient theater, which in so many other respects served as a model. "I could not help shuddering," says Corneille in the preface to his *Œdipe,* in speaking of the *Oedipus* of Sophocles,[42]

> when I considered it closely and a little more at leisure than I had done in selecting it. I recognized that what had passed for miraculous in those remote centuries might be an object of horror in ours, that the eloquent and curious account of how the unfortunate prince pierces his eyes, and the spectacle of the blood flowing over his face from those same eyes—that all this, which takes up the whole fifth act of the incomparable original, would offend the delicacy of our ladies. . . . I have tried to remedy these disorders. . . .

Because the Greek and the French tragedies played to radically different audiences, they differ radically in structure. Despite the many differences between them the Greek and the Christian-medieval theaters resemble one another and contrast with the French tragedy in their frank representation of human frailty. It becomes perfectly clear that the French theater audience could not have been "the people," but only polite society, *la cour et la ville.* A glance at any *préface* or at any polemic of the time suffices to show that the matters discussed, though treated in an easily intelligible and often superficial way, are addressed only to cultivated society. This aesthetic criticism, which spread through the whole of Europe and which, though its rule is very much shaken, still makes itself felt, came into being in French classicism—at the same time as the new lord of the theater, *le public.*

And now let us ask: What was the basis of the inherent unity of this "public"; how did it become a unified whole; and how did it arrive at its characteristic culture? In order to answer these questions, we must once again examine the two components, *la cour* and *la ville,* and try to ascertain how each of them came by the common culture.

The court of Louis XIV consisted almost entirely of nobles. The actual political power, to be sure, was in the hands of a few officials of largely bourgeois origin; but the social atmosphere of the court was created by the nobility. The history of this class, which developed from the military regime and economic order of feudalism, has often been recounted. In the course of the economic and military upheavals of the late Middle Ages and the Renaissance, it had gradually lost its function of governing and protecting the "people"; particularly in France, the unity of the state had been established in opposition to the nobles. They had preserved a traditional, largely psychological prestige, the most important posts in the military apparatus, and important class privileges of a fiscal and administrative nature; but they had lost the actual foundations of power. They had been unable to maintain the exclusive character of their caste—many members of the bourgeoisie had made their way into it by the purchase of noble estates, by marriage, by royal decree, and by outright usurpation. The lower limits remained fluid. With their power and offices, the nobles had also lost

the foundations of their wealth; many were impoverished and deeply in debt, and although they still had
sufficient prestige to obtain help in case of need, it no
longer derived from their own power but from the
favor of others, chiefly the king. Their class autonomy
was irrevocably lost; the king, on whose favor their
material welfare largely depended, allowed their class
as such no real power. This development had begun a
long time before the accession of Louis XIV; it is discernible as early as the fourteenth century, and the role
of the feudal nobility in the wars of religion and the
Fronde was a last vain, and rather muddled, attempt
at resistance. Richelieu had declared, particularly in
his *Testament politique,* that the nobility must be
saved; but he had no idea of restoring its original
feudal power. On the contrary, he wished to make it
an elite caste in the King's service. But this plan was
doomed to failure. The nobility remained barred from
any basic function in the state; it did not, as in Prussia,
become the organic administrative class—for the venality of offices and the long consolidated power of the
bourgeois *robe* prevented the nobles from obtaining a
monopoly on administrative positions. Louis XIV completed this development, destroying the provincial
power of the nobility by his appointment of intendants,
and compelling the nobles to live at court, which was
the only place where the members of this class, formerly independent and hostile to the central power,
could now find wealth, esteem, and employment—of a
military or decorative nature, or both. At court the
nobles showed their capacity for forming a society—
but they were unable to lend this society a definitely
aristocratic character, for they themselves had ceased
to be aristocrats in anything more than a formal and
negative sense.

Side by side with the economic and political development—though more slowly—a cultural change had taken place within the nobility. The culture of the medieval courts had disintegrated long before, while humanistic culture had been unable to make the conquest of the French nobility. At the beginning of the seventeenth century the nobles—to judge by a good many of their statements that have come down to us— were largely hostile to education, holding that a *gentilhomme* had no need to know anything but the trade of arms.[43] But this was to change in the course of the century. The idea, effective in Italy since the Renaissance, of a "natural" aristocracy based on cultivation and inherent worth, theoretically unconnected with birth though more readily accessible to the well born, for whom it represented an obligation, now came to France, but in a late form which laid greater stress on social than on individual perfection. This notion of a natural aristocracy had actually made its appearance in France a whole century before; it had been very much alive in the circle of Margaret of Navarre. But the turmoil and fanaticism of the religious wars, the peculiar character of the sons of Henry II, the final victory of the rustic Henry of Navarre—in short, the absence of a class that might have championed and sustained such an attitude, prevented it from maturing before the beginning of the seventeenth century. This social change took form in the salon of Madame de Rambouillet, and it was from there that its first influence radiated. Madame de Rambouillet was a granddaughter of the great Roman house of Savelli, and her social aptitudes were doubtless a heritage of the Italian Renaissance tradition. But she was, or became, a Frenchwoman; the form of society that she created was truly French and far removed from the Renaissance. In the place of the great hall of the secular and spiritual princes, the magnificent patrons of artists and poets, she created the *salon:*[44] a place where a group of men and women, essentially equal and having between them no ties of economic dependency, met on terms of social intimacy. Her circle comprised members of the highest aristocracy and the leading representatives of cultural life; it was *le rendez-vous de ce qu'il y avait de plus galant à la cour et de plus poli parmi les beaux-esprits du siècle.*[45] Though the *beaux-esprits* may have derived certain indirect advantages from frequenting the *salon,* they were far from the economic dependency characteristic of the Italian Renaissance—one need only think of the court of the house of Este; actually most of them were men of independent means.[46]

Thus the Hôtel de Rambouillet was the first home of the atmosphere which foreigners, down to our own century, have looked on as typical of French society, an atmosphere compounded of cultivation, equality, social warmth, and ease, adaptation of the individual's inner life to the socially appropriate, and the concealment of all unseemly depths. The Rambouillet *salon* regarded itself as aristocratic and so it was; it was an independent power, distinct from the court and the lower social groups, and this power rested in large part on the great names of those who frequented it. But the bearers of these great names had none of the haughty defiance of their feudal ancestors. In their relations with their cultured bourgeois friends, the sentiment of class hierarchy had dwindled into a barely perceptible, but on both sides carefully cultivated, keeping of distances. Yet what held this *salon* together was not its culture—that would be too modern and one-sided a view—but the much discussed and much defined notion of *honnêteté.* This was not a class ideal, for essentially it was not contingent on birth or on the manner of living of any particular caste. Such phrases as *un*

honnête homme aux Indes or *les honnêtes gens de l'antiquité*[47] show that the word referred to a purely personal ideal. In the course of the century, it came to be
applied to members of a larger and larger section of
society. Indeed, the concept of *honnêteté* had nothing
to do with class or economic position. Anyone could
become an *honnête personne* who was willing and able
to cultivate his inner and outer person in accordance
with the spirit of the times. The product was a man
cleansed of all particular qualities, no longer a member of a class, a profession, a religion, but precisely an
honnête homme. To be sure, this implied a recognition and observance of distances; an *honnête homme*
was expected to know himself, *se connaître,* and this
meant knowing his position in society; for the bourgeois *honnête homme* this self-knowledge was essential;
but if he possessed it, he was accepted as an equal in
the confraternity of *honnêtes hommes. Rien du poète
dans son commerce, et tout de l'honnête homme,* said
Saint-Simon, who was a good judge, in praise of Racine[48]—meaning that this poet of bourgeois origin
adapted himself perfectly to society, knew his place in
it, and was therefore an equal among equals. Here
then was an absolute ideal which directly concerned
the human person. True, it applied primarily to the
relations between human persons; but it was not restricted to any class. When Louis XIV began to govern,
he found this nobility which had lost its feudal class
instincts, and had preserved only a sense of its formal
and practical prestige. This is made clear by the self-
portrait of the young Marquis Acaste in *Le Misanthrope* (III, 1), part of which I have quoted above for
different reasons:

*Parbleu, je ne vois pas, lorsque je m'examine
Où prendre aucun sujet d'avoir l'âme chagrine.*

J'ai du bien, je suis jeune, et sors d'une maison
Qui se peut dire noble avec quelque raison;
Et je crois, par le rang que me donne ma race,
Qu'il est fort peu d'emplois dont je ne sois en passe;
Pour le cœur, dont surtout nous devons faire cas,
On sait, sans vanité, que je n'en manque pas. . . .

(Indeed, when I consider myself, I find no ground for
dismay. I am well off, I am young, and I come of a
family that is quite entitled to call itself noble. I
believe, in view of the rank conferred on me by my
lineage, that there are not many posts beyond my
reach. And as to the heart, which is what we should
value most, everyone knows, I can say without vanity,
that mine is in the right place. . . .)

What strikes us here is not so much the vanity (perhaps pardonable in a young man blessed by good fortune) as the total lack of seriousness, for if any such
quality were present it would surely be discernible in
a self-portrait of this kind. This lack of seriousness is
not a personal trait; it pertains to Acaste as a member
of his class. He is not serious because he has no voca-
tion springing from his membership in his class, no
function in life—though also, to be sure, because he
himself is not capable of remedying this deficiency. He
is not aware of it. He is well born enough to lay claim
to any position whatsoever; he is in favor with the
King, who will give him one when he sees fit. For the
present, Acaste lives in the void and expends his powers in play. He is available for everything; the only
value he is attached to is a *bienséance* devoid of content. He is a member of his class, and this membership
clings to him like a badge, meaningless, without economic or political or any other organic foundation,
but recognized by all. Like his class, he is without
function and prepared to serve, that is, to occupy any

decorative position "conforming to his station" that the King chooses to confer on him. The nobility is a class without a function, yet recognized as a privileged class and to all outward appearance occupying a position of real power. This results from the century's tendency to obscure the functional, organic realities, its penchant for the representational and the decorative. The same tendency accounts for the prevailing view of power as legitimate solely because it is established—a view which, had there been any discernible unity between function and power, could never have arisen in the radical form represented, for example, by Pascal. This same conception is basic in other moralists, such as La Bruyère, and underlies the generally accepted picture of the great of this earth, as presented in the tragedies. But this leads further than our present purposes require. Let us simply note that the nobility was a class that had no function, but bore the badge of power. So much for *la cour*.[49]

An analysis of *la ville* is far more difficult. We have already established that it was not the common people. The common people were silent in this century,[50] their voice would not be heard again for a long time to come. We have also established that even the *parterre* was not the common people. Nor were the *parterre* and the bourgeois tradesmen whom we have attempted to portray above by any means equivalent to *la ville*, which is a far broader concept. *La ville* was the grande bourgeoisie, the cultivated persons whose mere birth did not entitle them to be received at court. But only a part of the grande bourgeoisie still engaged in industry or commerce, and the other part is the more important. It is not easy to arrive at any concrete information about this other group, *la robe*, because the historical and sociological studies on the subject do not tell us what we want to know. The historians and students of government provide a general picture of the classes, their structure and hierarchy, but tell us little about the facts of their life; the economists speak of Colbertism, productive relations, and the financial administration, but all this in such general terms that we never find out how people actually lived. And relatively little attention has been given to the thin upper crust of the bourgeoisie which constituted the urban *public* and formed the dominant element in *la ville*. Groethuysen's well-documented *Les Origines de la France bourgeoise* starts from conditions in the eighteenth century; it presents a bourgeoisie active in industry and commerce, achieving awareness of its economic and moral importance and on its way to becoming the dominant class of society. But it was quite otherwise in the seventeenth century when at most we can discern the first furtive beginnings of bourgeois power—though, of course, as has often been shown (Wolters, Bergsträsser), the absolutist economic policy of Colbert in the seventeenth century was the foundation of the future development. In any event the dominant section of the grande bourgeoisie in the classical period did not consist of the self-confident businessmen who a century later led their class to political and cultural hegemony. Quite on the contrary. The strictly functional aspect of the bourgeoisie—its economic character, which it had asserted with moderation in earlier periods of French history, and on which in a later day it was to insist as the source of its power—was as far as possible forgotten or glossed over in the seventeenth century.

In this connection it is illuminating to note the social origins of the intellectual leaders of the day. Since the clergy was no longer the repository of cultural life and the intellectual leaders had to be recruited from the cultivated public, our findings are bound to throw some light on the social structure of *la ville*.

We find relatively few who definitely belonged to the old feudal aristocracy, and most of these, as well as their ideas and attitudes, belong to an earlier period; they are: Larochefoucauld, Bussy-Rabutin, Saint-Evremond, Madame de Sévigné, Balzac, Méré, Racan, Tristan L'Hermite, La Calprenède, Scudéry, and Saint-Cyran; the only later figure I can think of is Fénelon, and he is postclassical. The overwhelming majority are of bourgeois origin; most of these in turn were descended from the *robe* and many actually held positions identified with it. In this compilation I have —rightly, I hope—attached less importance to whether an individual bore a title of nobility or whether his family claimed noble descent than to his actual status in the period that concerns us. It must also be borne in mind that in the eyes of their contemporaries this group was far from monolithic; there were different classes of *robe* (*grande, moyenne, petite*) and various gradations within each class; in Paris certain quarters, such as the Marais, were inhabited by the *grande robe*, others were associated with the *petite robe* (Place Maubert); and I am not even sure that it is correct to designate all persons holding positions in the administration or judiciary as members of the *robe*. Vauban, in *La Dîme Royale,* makes a distinction between *Gens de Robe* [*qui sont*] . . . *Officiers de Justice, de Finance et de Police* and *Bourgeois . . . vivans de leurs Charges.* Nevertheless, as we shall show later on, the group has a certain homogeneous character for our purposes.

Here are the names in alphabetical order: Arnauld (office-holding aristocracy from Auvergne, of a prolific and highly respected family of great vitality known since the beginning of the sixteenth century); Boileau (father *greffier de la Grand' Chambre au Parlement de Paris*); Bossuet (office-holding aristocracy from Burgundy); Bourdaloue (family of officials from Bourges); Chapelain (father *conseiller garde-notes*); Conrart (father a strict Calvinist; I have been unable to discover his occupation, but he originally destined his son for a financial position); Corneille (family of officials from Rouen); Descartes (seems to have possessed a title of nobility, but according to Nicéron,[51] his father was a *conseiller au Parlement de Bretagne,* hence presumably *grande robe*); Furetière (started out as a lawyer); Gombertville (father a *boursier*—a kind of notary— *de la Chambre des Comptes*); La Bruyère (father secretary to the King, old family of officials; he himself was *trésorier du roi* at Caen, later a tutor in the house of Condé); La Fontaine (father *maître particulier des eux et forêts at Château-Thierry*); Le Maistre and his brother De Saci (father *maître de comptes;* Le Maistre himself a lawyer); Malebranche (father *secrétaire du roi et trésorier des cinq grosses fermes* under Richelieu, a very high and remunerative post in the finance administration); Malherbe (his family, it appears, belonged originally to the feudal aristocracy, but his father was *conseiller au présidial de Caen;* his wife was the widow of a *conseiller* and the daughter of a *président*); Massillon (father a notary at Hyères); Maynard (father *conseiller au Parlement de Toulouse*); Ménage (father *avocat du roi* at Angers); La Mothe le Vayer (according to Nicéron, came of a Le Mans family which for many years provided respected members of the *robe*); Nicole (father a lawyer at Chartres); Pascal (his father and Périer, his brother-in-law, were members of the *grande robe*); Gui Patin (family of lawyers, notaries, and *conseillers*); Patru (lawyer); Perrault (father *avocat au parlement;* he and his brother held high finance positions); Racine (the position of *contrôleur du grenier à sel*—an official in the administration of the salt monopoly—at La Ferté-Milon was hereditary in his family); Rotrou (family of officials from Normandy, his father a *rentier*); Scarron (father a *conseiller au parlement*); Sorel (father *procureur au parlement*); Vaugelas (ennobled family; his father was Favre, the celebrated jurist). A last, extremely small group, finally, comprises men whose fathers were still engaged in bourgeois occupations. These are Fléchier (family of small merchants); Molière (his father, a *marchand-tapissier,* purchased the post of *valet de chambre du roi*); Quinault (father a baker), and Voiture (father a wealthy wine merchant).

Here we may disregard the handful of nobles. The vast majority of the others were descended from the various categories of *robe*. To understand why this was so, let us recall that most official positions were venal and could be made hereditary on payment of certain fees. This practice had begun toward the end of the Middle Ages; after long struggles, it became prevalent in the sixteenth century when the office-holding bourgeoisie first achieved political, moral, and social weight; it was definitely legitimized and organized by the *édit de la Paulette* of 1604.[52] For fiscal and political reasons the monarchy encouraged this development despite its serious disadvantages and dangers,[53] and since the demand for positions was always very great, new ones were always being created. The purchasers came of the bourgeoisie, which had achieved unprecedented prosperity through the vast increase in the circulation of money and the resulting stimulation of production. Like those of many other periods and countries, these bourgeois were characterized by a desire to escape from their class and to stabilize their wealth. They wanted their children to enjoy a higher social rank and a

more exalted occupation than their own. They wished
to prevent them from risking their fortune in new
business ventures; the state was beginning to float loans
at a fixed rate of interest, and the *rentier* type was first
making its appearance. Spreading side by side with
prosperity, humanism and its ideal of *otium cum digni-
tate* also encouraged the flight of the bourgeois from
their class. The system of *survivances* gave rise to official dynasties, nepotism, a new consciousness of class.
The press of office seekers became such that the state
was scarcely able to satisfy the demand. It created posts
requiring little or no activity; along with charges
amounting to a real profession, there were purely decorative appointments that left their incumbents complete leisure—as had long been the case with many
positions in the Church and at court. Furthermore, the
economic situation of many families had changed. The
sharing of estates among many children, the capricious
treatment of *rentiers* by the state financial administration, and other circumstances had reduced the wealth
of certain families of the *grande bourgeoisie,* though
for the most part this meant only that their income was
no longer equal to their standard of living. But by now
these *grands bourgeois* had become *honnêtes gens,* to
whom it did not even occur to repair their fortunes by
business activity—instead, they sought the help of the
King or his entourage, more lucrative offices, pensions,
sinecures. They had become totally parasitic.

This phenomenon of mass flight from economic life
shows us a new aspect of *la ville,* which accounts for
what it had in common with *la cour.* Here again we
have a separation from the class base, from the organic
function of the economic group. The ideal of the
honnête homme, to which the upper bourgeoisie had
also come to aspire, was an ideal of universality, hostile
to all specific occupations. Of course, these remarks do

not pertain to the entire *robe;* the situation was not as clear and simple as all that. There were still whole groups and families that maintained a tradition of attachment to their work and class and provided excellent officials in the administration and judiciary apparatus; and indeed it was they who quietly conducted the actual business of the state. But they were few, they became more and more isolated as the century progressed, and they made no mark on the general social picture. The man who was interested in his occupation and knew something about it came to be regarded more and more as a crank, a fool, a petty and even contemptible sort of creature. When a judge, a lawyer, or a physician appears on the stage, it is always in a comic and repugnant role. If Dandin, the comic judge in Racine's *Les Plaideurs*—who, it might be mentioned, still had the *robe*'s class-conscious contempt for the parasitic aristocracy *Qu'est-ce qu'un gentilhomme? Un pilier d'antichambre . . .*)—if Dandin were an exception, if anywhere in the whole literature of the time a man devoted to his occupation were taken seriously, we should not be justified in citing Dandin as an example. But he is only a particularly successful portrait amid a whole gallery of similar figures. It is quite safe to say that the spirit of the times despised the practical activity of professional life; that an *honnête homme* was expected to conceal it and reduce it to a minimum and that a demeanor from which every last trace of it had been expelled was a great personal advantage—*rien du poète, tout de l'honnête homme.*[54] The turn from productive activity to officialdom was merely an expression of this attitude; in most cases the bourgeois chose a position because it offered social advantages in keeping with his wealth, not because he was fit for it or interested in it.[55]

Our most accessible source of information about the

attitudes of the upper bourgeoisie is Molière. Those of his plays that definitely take place in this milieu are: *L'Avare, Le Bourgeois Gentilhomme, Les Femmes savantes,* and *Le Malade imaginaire.*[56] All these families are very well off, and no one ever says a word about productive economic activity, for Harpagon's usury is the occupation of a *rentier.* We never learn the occupation of any of these bourgeois families—it seems safe to say that they no longer have any. The original source of a family's wealth is discussed only once, in *Le Bourgeois Gentilhomme,* where Madame Jourdain reminds her snobbish husband of it: "Is either of us descended entirely from *bonne bourgeoisie?* . . . Was your father not a merchant as much as mine . . . ?" And in the presence of their daughter: ". . . both her grandfathers sold cloth at the Porte Saint-Innocent." Monsieur Jourdain refuses to listen; he is bent on marrying his daughter to a noble at any cost and is overjoyed when told that his own father was a *gentilhomme* who procured cloth for his friends—against payment—just to be obliging. Monsieur Jourdain is an utter fool, a caricature, not at all typical of the *honnête homme bourgeois*—in his passion for nobility he forgets his limits, *il se méconnaît.*[57] But even Madame Jourdain, with all her sturdy bourgeois qualities, does not want her daughter to go back to the trading class; she wants for a son-in-law the bourgeois Cléonte, who in contrast to Monsieur Jourdain represents sound common sense. Cléonte, however, is far from practicing a trade. When Monsieur Jourdain asks him whether he is a *gentilhomme,* he replies:

> Sir, most men do not hesitate for long when asked that question; they are quite ready to say Yes. People have no scruple about accepting this title, and the use made of it today seems to authorize its theft. For my part,

I must own to you that my feelings in the matter are a little more fastidious. I believe that imposture of any kind is unworthy of an *honnête homme,* and that it is cowardly to disguise the condition in which God has brought us into the world, to adorn oneself in the eyes of the world with a purloined title, to attempt to pass for what one is not. Assuredly I was born of parents who have held honorable charges; I have secured the honor of six years service in arms, and I have fortune enough to give me a passable rank in society: but with all that, I have no desire to give myself a title to which others in my place would feel justified in laying claim; and so I tell you frankly that I am not a *gentilhomme.*

This young bourgeois knows his class, he is an *honnête homme qui se connaît.* He rejects the social climbing of such parvenus as Monsieur Jourdain (the second-generation rich whose fathers were still drapers). But he is equally far from the people, from those who work for a living, or from any concrete occupation. He does not tell us that his family is respected in the silk industry or the wine trade; no, *ils on tenu des charges honorables;* he himself served for six years as an officer; and he has sufficient wealth *pour tenir dans le monde un rang assez passable.* He is a typical grandson; with a little caution, one can transpose the social type he represents to Germany before the First World War. Except that in Germany this type was not the rule; a native bourgeois energy usually won out, drawing the young men of the grande bourgeoisie back to economic activity and the corresponding attitudes. In France more than a century before the Revolution it was otherwise; flight from economic life was the rule. Any thought of concrete economic activity, any suggestion of a bourgeois attitude is inconceivable in this young man. His class, like the nobility of Acaste in *Le Misanthrope,* is *un rang qu'on tient dans le monde.* Like his parents, he will purchase or inherit a *charge honorable.* The behavior of young Cléante in *L'Avare* is also illuminating in this connection: What does he do to free himself from the oppression of his miserly father? He borrows from usurers in his father's name, *pour donner furieusement dans le marquis.* In Molière's well-to-do bourgeois families, economic activity, working for a living, are regarded as something base that one does not talk about. They appear only in Harpagon, in an illegitimate and utterly repellent form; wealth is something static, something fixed and immutable that just happens to be there. The only way in which Molière's young men know how to obtain money is by swindling their fathers.

But education stands in high esteem. One should not be misled by Mônsieur Jourdain's grotesque lessons; he is an upstart who does not know how an *honnête homme* of his day goes about acquiring an education. The essence of the matter is revealed in *Les Femmes savantes,* and here again we should not be misled by Chrysale's famous outburst. With his base egotism— *ma viande, mon pot, mon rôt, mes rabats*—he is as comic a figure as Trissotin, and Philaminte's exclamation: *Quelle bassesse, o ciel, et d'âme et de langage* is perfectly in keeping with the spirit of the time. As usual Molière's view is in the middle. Henriette and Clitandre represent it, and Clitandre expresses it several times (I, 3, and above all in his argument with Trissotin, IV, 3). This ideal of refinement and good taste resulted from immersion in the humanistic culture that had spread with the spread of prosperity, taking hold of the nobility as well as the upper bourgeoisie, while humanism itself turned from erudition to education. In France this development seems to have started with

Amyot's Plutarch—"thanks to it, we are not afraid to speak and write today; the ladies instruct the schoolmasters in it; it is our breviary," wrote Montaigne.[58] Under the influence of Cartesianism the new culture came to include a certain knowledge of physics and even philosophy; the dividing lines between aristocratic, learned, and middle-class patterns of thought were gradually broken down; the people were silent and a cultivated society of nobles and well-to-do bourgeois, having molded learning to its purposes, became the sole repository of cultural life: this was *la cour et la ville.*

In his *Roman bourgeois* Furetière gives us still another picture of the parasitic bourgeoisie; no doubt the author's petty and spiteful temperament plays a part, but in any case the picture is hardly attractive. Furetière introduces us to a circle of base, grasping, grossly materialistic petits bourgeois. Here, to be sure, money is "earned," but not by honest productive effort, not by industry and commerce, but by parasitic guile and chicanery. The characters are lawyers who get rich at the expense of their clients; all are totally unscrupulous and many lack the slightest training or aptitude for their profession. The maneuvers by which they arrived at their position, the dark deals and base intrigues, may be distorted and exaggerated; but there must be some amount of truth in the picture, for even exaggeration requires a certain foundation of authenticity. A few passages throw a considerable light on the questions that concern us here. In the beginning of the book we find a scale of dowries: *Tariffe ou évaluation des partis sortables pour faire facilement des mariages* —indicating what sort of match a young lady in each of nine dowry classes can expect to make. Merchants appear only in the two lowest classes, and even then in competition with the lowest classes of *robe;* for the higher brackets only members of the *robe* are considered suitable, and the list gives us an idea of the relative prestige attaching to the various *charges*.[59] This list fully supports our survey of the occupations of the families of writers. Only the office-holders counted as bourgeoisie, as *ville;* those engaged in productive occupations were declassed. Even so, I have no doubt that the "public" included many who were engaged in economic life, as for example the *marchands de la rue Saint-Denis;* but these were without consciousness of their class; they looked upward, and whenever possible purchased a *charge honorable* for their son. Those members of the bourgeoisie who figured in the "public" were parasitic and without function—at least in their desires and ideals, and often in fact. The difference between bourgeoisie and nobility, between *gens du commun* and *gens du bel air* is often stressed in the *Roman bourgeois,* but only in the sense that the petit bourgeois characters of the book do not master the lofty tone in social relations and the gallant forms of love play that have come to be taken for granted in the higher spheres; their class character is indicated only negatively. In this book there is no sign of any positive and pondered bourgeois self-awareness that might be contrasted with the elegant tone, the munificence, the gallantry, and frivolity of the nobles. On the contrary, the young men of this middle class succumb without resistance to the ideals they regard as aristocratic, although by then these ideals had ceased to be noble and had become purely social: an interest in the subtleties of fashion, a taste for gallant verses, and above all, love in the Precious manner. A cavalier gives a copy of *Astrée* to a young, inexperienced girl who has hitherto been protected from all social life, and in a twinkling her life is made over; she herself becomes Astrée, while her cavalier plays the part of Céladon.

The Precious novels were of the utmost importance in the formation of the cultivated bourgeoisie; by way of these bucolic idyls, the young bourgeois learned to ponder and dwell on his own feelings, to derive a sense of dignity from them, and to yearn for a completely detached life devoted to love alone. They, too, helped to foster the state of mind which despises concrete reality as unworthy of a man of noble feelings, but which nevertheless aspired to wealth and a life on the social heights, where alone the paradise of sublime love seemed possible of attainment.

We sum up. *La cour et la ville* were a unit which took form in the course of the century and which may already be termed a "public" in the modern sense. The two parts of this unit were to be sure distinct in formal rank, but the dividing line between them was repeatedly crossed, and above all each part had lost its authentic foundations. The nobility as such had lost its function and had ceased to be anything more than the King's entourage; the bourgeoisie, or at least the part of it that may be termed *ville,* was also alienated from its original function as an economic class. With their parasitic absence of function and common cultural ideal, *la cour et la ville* merged into a self-contained, homogeneous society.

VICO AND AESTHETIC HISTORISM

VICO AND AESTHETIC HISTORISM

Modern critics of art or of literature consider and admire, with the same preparedness for understanding, Giotto and Michelangelo, Michelangelo and Rembrandt, Rembrandt and Picasso, Picasso and a Persian miniature; or Racine and Shakespeare, Chaucer and Alexander Pope, the Chinese lyrics and T. S. Eliot. The preference they may give to one or the other of the various periods or artists is no longer imposed upon them by certain aesthetic rules or judgments dominating the feelings of all our contemporaries, but such preferences are merely personal predilections originating from individual taste or individual experiences. A critic who would condemn the art of Shakespeare or of Rembrandt or even the drawings of the ice age primitives as being of bad taste because they do not conform to the aesthetic standards established by classical Greek or Roman theory would not be taken seriously by anybody.

This largeness of our aesthetic horizon is a consequence of our historical perspective; it is based on historism, i.e., on the conviction that every civilization and every period has its own possibilities of aesthetic perfection; that the works of art of the different peoples and periods, as well as their general forms of life, must be understood as products of variable individual con-

ditions, and have to be judged each by its own development, not by absolute rules of beauty and ugliness.
General and aesthetic historism is a precious (and also
a very dangerous) acquisition of the human mind; it is
a comparatively recent one. Before the sixteenth century, the historical and geographical horizon of the
Europeans was not large enough for such conceptions;
and even in the Renaissance, the seventeenth, and the
beginning of the eighteenth century, the first moves
toward historism were overbalanced by currents which
worked against it; especially by the admiration of
Greek and Roman civilization, which focused the attention on classical art and poetry; these became models to be imitated, and nothing is more contrary to
aesthetic historism than imitation of models. It pro-
motes absolute standards and rules of beauty, and
creates an aesthetic dogmatism such as was admirably
achieved by the French civilization of the time of Louis
XIV. Besides this there was another current in the sixteenth and seventeenth centuries acting against historical perspective: the revival of the ancient concept of
absolute human nature. The sudden enlargement of
the horizon, the discovery of the variety and relativity
of human religions, laws, customs, and tastes which
occurred in the Renaissance, did not lead, in most
cases, to historical perspective, that is to say, to an
attempt to understand them all and to acknowledge
their relative merits; it led, on the contrary, to the rejection of all of them, to a struggle against the variety
of historical forms, to a struggle against history, and to
a powerful revival of the concept of true or original or
uncorrupted absolute human nature as opposed to history. History seemed to be nothing but "the actions
and institutions of men," arbitrary, erroneous, perni-
cious, and even fraudulent. The worthlessness of such
institutions seemed to be proved sufficiently by their

variety; and the task of mankind seemed to be to replace them all by absolute standards according to the
law of nature. There were indeed very different opinions about the nature of this nature; between those
who identified human nature with the primitive unciv-
ilized origins of mankind, and those who, on the contrary, identified nature with enlightened reason, there
were all kinds of shades and gradations. But the static
and absolute character of this human nature, as opposed to the changes of history, is common to all these
theories of human nature and natural law. Montes-
quieu introduced a certain amount of historical perspective by his explanation of the variety of human
forms of government, by climate and other material
conditions; with the ideas of Diderot and Rousseau the
concept of general and of human nature became
strongly dynamic; but it was still a nature opposed to
history.

Aesthetic historism, followed by general historism,
practically originated in the second half of the eighteenth century, as a reaction against the European predominance of French classicism; the preromantic and
romantic currents created it and spread it all over
Europe. The most vigorous impulse came from Germany, from the so-called Storm and Stress group of the
1770's, from the first works of Herder and Goethe and
their friends; later from the Schlegel brothers and the
other German romantics. Herder and his followers
started from the conception of the original folk genius
as the creator of true poetry; in strong opposition to
all theories which based poetry and art on highly developed civilization, good taste, imitation of models,
and well-defined rules, they believed that poetry is the
work of free instinct and imagination, and that it is
most spontaneous and genuine in the early periods of
civilization, in the youth of mankind, when instinct,

imagination, and oral tradition were stronger than reason and reflection, when "poetry was the natural language of men"; hence their predilection for folk songs and folk tales, their theory that ancient epic poetry (parts of the Bible, Homer, the epic poetry of the Middle Ages) were not consciously composed by individuals, but had grown up and were synthetized unconsciously from many anonymous contributions—songs or tales—originating from the depth of the folk genius; hence finally their conviction that even in modern times true poetry can be reborn only from a return to its eternal source, the folk genius, with its unconscious and instinctive development of traditions. These men conceived history, not as a series of exterior facts and conscious actions of men, not as a series of mistakes and frauds, but as a subconscious, slow, and organic evolution of "forces," which were considered as manifestations of the Divinity. They admired the variety of historical forms as the realization of the infinite variety of the divine spirit, manifesting itself through the genius of the various peoples and periods. The divinization of history led to an enthusiastic research into the individual historical and aesthetic forms, to the attempt to understand them all by their own individual conditions of growth and development, to a contemptuous rejection of all aesthetic systems based on absolute and rationalistic standards. Thus, the preromantic and romantic movement was practically the origin of modern historism and of modern historical sciences: history of literature, of language, of art, but also of political forms, of law, and so on, conceived as an organic evolution of various individual forms. The origin of modern historism is, therefore, closely linked with the preromantic and "Nordic" admiration for primitive and early forms of civilization, and, of course, strongly influenced by Rousseau's concept of original human nature; the origins of mankind are seen with a certain idyllic, lyrical, and pantheistic connotation. But, whereas Rousseau's concept was, on the whole, revolutionary—nature directed against history, because history was responsible for the inequality of men and the corruption of society—the romantics introduced the conception of natural and organic evolution into history itself; they developed an evolutionary conservatism, based on the traditions of the folk genius, directed as much against the rationalistic forms of absolutism as against rationalistic tendencies toward revolutionary progress. Their organic conservatism resulted from their prevailing interest in the individual roots and forms of the folk genius, in folklore, national traditions, and the national individuality in general. Although this interest was extended to foreign national forms in the literary and scientific activities of the romantics, it led many of them, especially in Germany, to an extremely nationalistic attitude toward their own fatherland, which they considered as the synthesis and supreme realization of folk genius. Contemporary circumstances and events—the political disaggregation of Germany, the French Revolution, Napoleon's domination—contributed to the development of such feelings.

Now, it is one of the most astonishing facts in the history of ideas that very similar principles had been conceived and published half a century before their first preromantic appearance by an elderly Neapolitan scholar, Giambattista Vico (1668-1744), in his *Scienza Nuova,* which appeared first in 1725—by a man totally ignorant of all the conditions which, fifty years later, fostered and promoted such ideas. Shaftesbury's and Rousseau's influence, the vitalistic trend of certain eighteenth-century biologists, French and English poetry of sensibility, the cult of Ossian and German pietism—all these influences and movements which created the preromantic milieu developed long after Vico's death. He did not even know Shakespeare; his education had been classical and rationalistic, and he had no opportunity to become interested in Nordic folklore. The Storm and Stress movement was specifically Nordic in its aspect: it originated in a milieu of youthful liberty, it was promoted by a whole group of young men bound together by the same enthusiastic feelings. Vico was a solitary old professor at the University of Naples who had taught Latin figures of speech all his life and had written hyperbolical eulogies for the various Neapolitan viceroys and other important personalities. Nor had he any appreciable influence upon the preromantic and romantic movements. The difficulties of his style and the baroque atmosphere of his book, an atmosphere totally different from romanticism, covered it with a cloud of impenetrability. Even the few Germans who, in the second part of the eighteenth century, happened to see it and to turn over its leaves, men like Hamann, Friedrich Heinrich Jacobi, and Goethe, failed to recognize its importance and to penetrate to its leading ideas. It is true that the continuous efforts of modern scholars to establish a link between Vico and Herder have finally met with some success, since Professor Robert T. Clark has shown the probability that Herder was inspired, in some of his ideas concerning language and poetry, by the notes to Denis's German translation of Macpherson. Denis had appropriated these notes from Cesarotti, an Italian translator of Ossian who was well acquainted with the corresponding ideas of Vico.[1] Professor Clark's discovery is certainly interesting and important, but such a casual, indirect, and incomplete contact—Herder did not even mention the name of Vico, which meant nothing to him—is almost tragically incongruous with the general importance Vico

should have had for the preromantic and romantic
writers. He should have been one of their acknowledged and admired forerunners just as, or even more
than, were Shaftesbury and Rousseau. But even in
Vico's own country, in Italy, nobody really understood
his ideas. To put it in the words of Max Harold Fisch,
in the excellent introduction to his (and Thomas Goddard Bergin's) recent American translation of Vico's
autobiography: none of those "who borrowed this or
that from Vico in the pre-revolutionary period was able
to free himself altogether from the prevailing rational-
ist temper, to grasp Vico's thought as an integral whole,
or even to place himself at its living center." [2]

Vico arrived very late at the maturity of his ideas.
Neither the Epicurean tendencies of his youth nor the
Cartesianism which prevailed in Naples during his
later life—which he opposed passionately without suc-
ceeding in freeing himself from its powerful attraction
—nor, finally, the rationalistic theories of natural law
were a favorable background for his approach to history. Throughout a great part of his life, he tried to
find an epistemological base for his ideas, against the
Cartesian contempt of history. He was in his fifties
when he finally succeeded in finding a form for his
theory of cognition which satisfied him, and even filled
him with enthusiasm. In this ultimate form, the theory
says that there is no knowledge without creation; only
the creator has knowledge of what he has created himself; the physical world—*il mondo della natura*—has
been created by God; therefore only God can understand it; but the historical or political world, the
world of mankind—*il mondo delle nazioni*—can be
understood by men, because men have made it. I have
no time now to discuss the theological implications of
this much debated theory, considered in its relations
with Vico's conception of Divine Providence. For our

purpose, it is sufficient to stress the fact that Vico had achieved by this theory the predominance of the historical sciences, based on the certitude that men can understand men, that all possible forms of human life and thinking, as created and experienced by men, must be found in the potentialities of the human mind (*dentro le modificazioni della nostra medesima mente umana*); that therefore we are capable of re-evoking human history from the depth of our own consciousness.

The impulse to this theory of cognition was given to Vico undoubtedly by his own historical discoveries. He had no scientific knowledge of primitive civilizations, and a very incomplete and vague knowledge of the Middle Ages; he was supported only by his scholarship in classical philology and Roman law. It is almost a miracle that a man, at the beginning of the eighteenth century in Naples, with such material for his research, could create a vision of world history based on the discovery of the magic character of primitive civilization. Certainly, he was inspired by the theories of natural law, by Spinoza, Hobbes, and especially by Grotius; or better, he was inspired by his opposition to their theories. Still, there are few similar examples in the history of human thought of isolated creation due to such an extent to the particular quality of the author's mind. He combined an almost mystical faith in the eternal order of human history with a tremendous power of productive imagination in the interpretation of myth, ancient poetry, and law.

In his view, the first men were neither innocent and happy beings living in accordance with an idyllic law of nature, nor terrible beasts moved only by the purely material instinct of self-preservation. He also rejected the concept of primitive society as founded by reason and common sense in the form of mutual agreement by

contract. For him, primitive men were orginally solitary nomads living in orderless promiscuity within the
chaos of a mysterious and for this very reason horrible
nature. They had no faculties of reasoning; they only
had very strong sensations and a strength of imagination such as civilized men can hardly understand.
When, after the deluge, the first thunderstorm broke
out, a minority of them, terror-struck by thunder and
lightning, conceived a first form of religion, which
modern scholars would call animistic: they personified
nature, their imagination created a world of magic
personifications, a world of living deities expressing
their might and their will by the natural phenomena;
and this minority of primitive men, in order to understand the will of the deities, to appease their wrath and
to win their support, created a system of fantastic and
magic ceremonies, formulas and sacrifices which governed all their life. They established sanctuaries at certain fixed places and became settled; hiding their sexual
relations as a religious taboo, they became monoga-
mous, thus founding the first families: primitive magic
religion is the base of social institutions. It is also the
origin of agriculture; the settlers were the first who
cultivated the soil. The primitive society of isolated
families is strongly patriarchal; the father is priest and
judge; by his exclusive knowledge of the magic ceremonies, he has absolute power over all the members of
his family; and the sacred formulas according to which
he rules them are of extreme severity; these laws are
strictly bound to the ritual wording, ignoring flexibil-
ity and consideration of special circumstances. Vico
called the life of these primitive fathers a severe poem;
they had huge bodies, and called themselves giants,
gigantes, sons of the Earth, because they were the first
to bury their dead and to worship their memory: the
first nobility. Their conceptions and expressions were

inspired by personifications and images; the mental order in which they conceived the surrounding world and created their institutions was not rational, but magic and fantastic. Vico calls it poetic; they were poets by their very nature; their wisdom, their metaphysics, their laws, all their life was "poetic." This is the first age of mankind, the golden age (golden because of the harvests), the age of the gods.

The development from the first to the second, the heroic age, is mainly political and economic. Stationary life and family constitution had given to the minority of settlers a superiority of wealth, material power, and religious prestige over the remnant of nomads, who finally were obliged to have recourse to the families of the fathers for protection and better living conditions; they were accepted as labor-slaves, as dependent members of the family of the first fathers or "heroes"; they were not admitted to the ritual ceremonies, and consequently had no human rights, no legal matrimony, no legitimate children, no property. But after a certain time the slaves or *famuli* began to rebel; a revolutionary movement developed, religious as well as social, for participation in the ceremonies, in legal rights and property. This movement obliged the isolated fathers to unite for defense, and to constitute the first communities, the heroic republics. They were oligarchical states, where religious, political, and economic power was entirely in the hands of the heroes; by maintaining the secrecy and inviolability of the divine mysteries they opposed all innovations in religion, law, and political structure. They preserved during this second period (which still was mentally "poetic" in the sense Vico uses this word) their narrow-minded virtue, their cruel discipline, and their magic formalism, still unable and unwilling to act by rationalistic considerations, symbolizing their life and their insti-

tutions in mythical concepts and strongly believing
themselves to be of a higher nature than the rest of men.
But rationalistic forms of mind, promoted by the revolutionary leaders of the plebeians (the former *famuli*),
developed more and more. Step by step the plebeians
tore away from the heroes their rights and prerogatives.
With the final victory of the plebeians begins the third
period of history, the age of men, a rationalistic and
democratic period, where imagination and poetry have
lost their creative power, where poetry is only an em-
bellishment of life and an elegant pastime, where all
men are considered as equals and are governed by elas-
tic and liberal religions and laws.[3] There is no doubt
about the striking similarity between Vico's ideas and
those of Herder and his followers. The poetical irra-
tionalism and the creative imagination of primitive
men are concepts common to both; both say that primitive men were poets by their very nature, that their
language, their conception of nature and history, their
entire life was poetry; both considered enlightened rationalism as unpoetical. But the concept of poetry, the
basic concept, is entirely different. Vico admired his
primitive giants and heroes as much as, perhaps even
more than, Herder loved and cultivated the folk genius. Their power of imagination and expression, the
concrete realism of their sublime metaphoric language,
the unity of concept pervading all their life became
for this poor old professor the model of creative greatness. He even admired—with an admiration so overwhelming that it proved to be stronger than his horror
—the terrible cruelty of their magic formalism. These
last words—the terrible cruelty of their magic formalism—well illustrate the immense discrepancy between
his concepts and those of Herder. Herder's conception
of the youth of mankind had grown on the ground of
Rousseau's theory of original nature; it had been nour-

ished and inspired by folk songs and folk tales; it is not political. The motive of magic animism is not entirely absent from his concepts, but it does not dominate, and it is not developed to its concrete implications and consequences. He saw the original state of mankind as a state of nature, and nature, for him, was liberty: liberty of feeling, of instinct, of inspiration, absence of laws and institutions, in striking contrast to the laws, conventions, and rules of rationalized society. He would never have conceived the idea that primitive imagination created institutions more severe and ferocious, boundaries more narrow and insurmountable than any civilized society can possibly do. But that is Vico's idea; it is the very essence of his system. The aim of primitive imagination, in his view, is not liberty, but, on the contrary, establishment of fixed limits, as a psychological and material protection against the chaos of the surrounding world. And later on, mythical imagination serves as the base of a political system and as a weapon in the struggle for political and economic power. The ages of the gods and the heroes, with their all pervading "poetry," are not at all poetical in the romantic sense, although, in both cases, poetry means imagination opposed to reason. The imagination of the folk genius produces folklore and traditions; the imagination of the giants and heroes produces myths which symbolize institutions according to the eternal law of Divine Providence. In Vico's system the old contrast of natural against positive law, of *physis* against *thesis,* of original nature against human institutions, becomes meaningless; Vico's poetical age, the golden age, is not an age of natural freedom, but an age of institutions. It is true that romantic conservatism also was very fond of institutions slowly and "organically" developed by the traditions of the folk genius—but these were of

another kind, and had another atmosphere than the
magic formalism of the heroes.

It is easy to show that Vico, long before Herder and
the romantics, discovered their most fertile aesthetic
concept, the concept of folk genius. He was the first
who tried to prove that primitive poetry is not the
work of individual artists, but was created by the whole
society of the primitive peoples, who were poets by
their very nature. In his third book, on "the discovery
of the true Homer," long before the German philolo-
gist Friedrich August Wolf, he developed the theory
that Homer was not an individual poet, but a myth, or,
as he puts it, a "poetical character" symbolizing the
rhapsodes or popular singers who wandered through
the Greek towns singing the deeds of the gods and the
heroes—and that *Iliad* and *Odyssey* were not originally
coherent works, but that they are composed of many
fragments from different periods of Greek early history; that they have been transmitted to us in a form
already altered and corrupted; but that to those who
are able to interpret them, they tell the history of
Greek primitive civilization. He thus anticipated the
famous romantic theory of popular epic poetry as a
product of the folk genius, a theory which dominated
philological research during a great part of the nineteenth century, and which still is very influential.

But Vico did not show any special interest in the
folk genius of the different individual peoples. His aim
was to establish eternal laws—the laws of Divine Providence which govern history: an evolution of human
civilization through distinct stages, an evolution which
would develop again and again, in eternal cycles,
wherever men should live. His suggestive analysis of
the different periods stresses their individual aspect
only in order to prove that they are typical stages of

this evolution; and although he occasionally admitted
that there exist some variants within the development
of the different peoples and societies, the study of
these variants would have seemed to him a matter of
minor importance. The romantics, on the contrary,
were chiefly interested in the individual forms of the
historical phenomena; they tried to understand the
particular spirit, to taste the specific flavor of the different periods as well as of the various peoples. They
studied the Scottish, English, Spanish, Italian, French,
German "folk genius" and many others; the understanding of the various organic popular developments
was the very center of their critical activities. It was
this impulse focused at individual forms of life and
art which proved so fertile for the historical sciences
in the nineteenth century, and which introduced into
them the spirit of historical perspective, as I tried to
explain on the first pages of this paper.

In this movement of early European historism,
Vico's ideas did not play an important part; his work
was not sufficiently known. It seems to me that this is
due not only to a casual combination of unfavorable
circumstances, but primarily to the fact that his vision
of human history lacked some of the most important
elements of romantic historism, and possessed others
which could hardly be understood and appreciated in
the preromantic and early romantic period. The slow
process of his gradual discovery in Europe began in the
1820's; later in the nineteenth century his influence
still remained sporadic, and many leading textbooks of
history of philosophy did not even mention his name.
But in the last forty years this has changed; his name
and his ideas have become important and familiar to
an ever increasing number of European and American
scholars and authors; the admirable activity Croce and
Nicolini devoted to the publication and interpretation

of his work met with considerable and steadily growing success. Some of his basic ideas seem to have acquired their full weight only for our time and our generation; as far as I know, no great author has been as much impressed by his work as James Joyce. There are, as it seems to me, three main ideas which are and may prove to be in future of great significance for our conceptions of aesthetics and history.

First, his discovery of the magic formalism of primitive men, with its power to create and to maintain institutions symbolized by myth; it includes a conception of poetry which has, undoubtedly, some relationship to modern forms of artistic expression. The complete unit of magic "poetry" or myth with political structure in primitive society, the interpretation of myths as symbols of political and economic struggles and developments, the concept of concrete realism in primitive language and myth are extremely suggestive of certain modern tendencies. By the word "tendencies," I do not allude to certain parties or countries, but to trends of thought and feeling spread all over our world.

The second point is Vico's theory of cognition. The entire development of human history, as made by men, is potentially contained in the human mind, and may therefore, by a process of research and re-evocation, be understood by men. The re-evocation is not only analytic; it has to be synthetic, as an understanding of every historical stage as an integral whole, of its genius (its *Geist,* as the German romantics would have said), a genius pervading all human activities and expressions of the period concerned. By this theory, Vico created the principle of historical understanding, entirely unknown to his contemporaries; the romantics knew and practiced this principle, but they never found such a powerful and suggestive epistemological base for it.

Finally, I want to stress his particular conception of

historical perspective; it can best be explained by his interpretation of human nature. Against all contemporary theorists, who believed in an absolute and unchanging human nature as opposed to the variety and changes of history, Vico created and passionately maintained the concept of the historical nature of men. He identified human history and human nature, he conceived human nature as a function of history. There are many passages in the *Scienza Nuova*[4] where the word *natura* should best be translated by "historical development" or "stage of historical development." Divine Providence makes human nature change from period to period, and in each period the institutions are in full accordance with the human nature of the period; the distinction between human nature and human history disappears; as Vico puts it, human history is a permanent Platonic state. This sounds rather ironical in a man who did not believe in progress, but in a cyclical movement of history. However, Vico was not ironical; he meant it in earnest.

THE AESTHETIC DIGNITY OF
THE "FLEURS DU MAL"

THE AESTHETIC DIGNITY OF THE "FLEURS DU MAL"

SPLEEN

Quand le ciel bas et lourd pèse comme un couvercle
Sur l'esprit gémissant en proie aux longs ennuis,
Et que de l'horizon embrassant tout le cercle
Il nous verse un jour noir plus triste que les nuits;

Quand la terre est changée en un cachot humide,
Où l'Espérance, comme une chauve-souris,
S'en va battant les murs de son aile timide
Et se cognant la tête à des plafonds pourris;

Quand la pluie étalant ses immenses traînées
D'une vaste prison imite les barreaux,
Et qu'un peuple muet d'infâmes araignées
Vient tendre ses filets au fond de nos cerveaux,

Des cloches tout à coup sautent avec furie
Et lancent vers le ciel un affreux hurlement,
Ainsi que des esprits errants et sans patrie
Qui se mettent à geindre opiniâtrement.

—Et de longs corbillards, sans tambour ni musique,
Défilent lentement dans mon âme; l'Espoir,
Vaincu, pleure, et l'Angoisse atroce, despotique,
Sur mon crâne incliné plante son drapeau noir.

(When the low, heavy sky weighs like a lid

On a spirit moaning beneath endless troubles
And, blocking off the whole horizon,
Decants a day more dismal than night;

When the earth is changed into a damp dungeon
Where Hope like a timid bat
Flaps her wings against the walls
And dashes her head against the moldy ceiling;

When the long lines of rain
Are like the bars of a vast prison
And a silent swarm of loathsome spiders
Spin their nets at the bottom of my brain,

Suddenly the bells leap out in a fury
And fling a hideous howling at the heavens,
Like homeless wandering spirits
Whimpering disconsolately.

And a long line of hearses without drums or music,
Files slowly through my soul; Hope vanquished weeps
And vile despotic Dread
Plants her black flag over my bowed skull.)

This poem is all of one movement. Actually, despite
the period after the fourth stanza, it seems to consist of
a single sentence; made up of three temporal dependent clauses, each taking up a whole stanza, each beginning with *quand,* and of a main clause with several
subdivisions, which unfolds in the last two stanzas.
The alexandrine meter makes it clear that this is a
serious poem, to be spoken slowly and gravely; it contains allegorical figures written in capital letters, *Espérance, Espoir, Angoisse;* and we also find epithets
and other rhetorical figures in the classical style (*de
son aile timide*). The syntactical unity, the grave
rhythm, and the rhetorical figures combine to lend the
poem an atmosphere of somber sublimity, which is
perfectly consonant with the deep despair it expresses.

The temporal clauses, describing a rainy day with low, heavy hanging clouds, are replete with metaphors: the sky like a heavy lid closing off the horizon, leaving us without prospect in the darkness; the earth like a damp dungeon; Hope like a fluttering bat caught in the moldering masonry; the threads of rain like the bars of a prison; and inside us a mute swarm of loathsome spiders, spinning their nets. All these figures symbolize dull, deepening despair. And there is an insistence about them which, if you submit to their spell, seems to exclude any possibility of a happier life. The *quand* loses its temporal meaning and rings out like a threat; we begin with the poet to doubt whether a sunny day will ever dawn again; for Hope, the poor bat, is also imprisoned and has lost touch with the world beyond the clouds—is there any such world? Even a reader unfamiliar with Baudelaire's other poems, who does not know how often he evokes the barred horizon, the damp and moldering dungeon of hell, who does not know how little use the sun is to him when it does happen to be shining, will grasp the irrevocable hopelessness of the situation from these three stanzas alone. Hopeless horror has its traditional place in literature; it is a special form of the sublime; we find it, for example, in some of the tragic poets and historians of antiquity, and of course we find it in Dante; it can lay claim to the highest dignity.

But in the first stanzas we already find things that seem hardly compatible with the dignity of the sublime. A modern reader barely notices them, he has long been accustomed to this style, established by Baudelaire, in which many poets, each in his own way, have subsequently made themselves at home. But Baudelaire's contemporaries, even those who had grown used to the daring of the romantics, must have been startled if not horrified. In the very first line the sky is compared to a lid, the lid of a pot or perhaps of a coffin—the former is more likely, for in another poem, *"Le Couvercle,"* Baudelaire writes:

> *Le Ciel! couvercle noir de la grande marmite*
> *Où bout l'imperceptible et vaste Humanité.*

(The sky! black lid of the great kettle
Where humanity simmers, vast and imperceptible.)

To be sure, Victor Hugo had proclaimed years before that the difference between noble and common words was done away with, but he had not gone so far, and much less had Alfred de Vigny, who of all the romantics was perhaps the most given to the tone of sublime horror. Of course damp moldering dungeons, bats and spiders, are perfectly in keeping with the romantic style, but only as properties in historical novels and plays, not in the sharp immediate present, not right beside or even inside the poet, and yet symbols for all that. The last word is *cerveaux,* a medical term. Clearly no realistic imitation is intended; on the contrary, the image of spiders in the brain is unrealistic and symbolic; but that makes it all the more degrading, for with spiders in his brain the suffering, despairing poet is denied the inward dignity conferred by such words as *âme* or *pensée.*

The three stanzas introduced by *quand* present a heavy silence. The fourth, which begins the main clause, brings in a sudden clamor: furious bells leap out and fling a hideous howling at the sky. Bells that leap furiously and howl at the sky! Anything more violent and outrageous is scarcely imaginable; such a combination offends against every traditional notion of the dignity of the sublime. True, *hurler* had been employed by the romantics in an orgiastic sense;[1] it seems to have been fashionable with certain literary circles

in the forties; but combinations of this sort occur no-
where else. Church bells that howl and leap with fury:
seventy years later such an image would have been
termed surrealistic. And, it must be remembered, we
are not on the style-level of satire, where one might
speak lightly of "clattering bells," but in an atmosphere of profound seriousness and bitter torment, and
therefore on the style-level of the tragic and sublime.
In the next lines the bells proceed to emit sounds that
might be characterized as a persistent blubbering
whimper; *geindre* is a childish blubbering, furious,
meaningless, and ignored; no one hears the homeless
spirits. And while this absurd hubbub is still raging,
the last stanza begins. Once again there seems to be
utter silence, the procession of hearses, *sans tambour
ni musique,* draws slowly through the poet's soul—
this time it is the soul, *mon âme,* whose last strength is
exhausted by the sight (a procession of memories, a
wasted life laden with guilt). Hope has given up looking for a way out; she is weeping; hideous Dread hoists
her black flag over the bowed skull, and so this magnificent poem ends. As a picture in the grand style of
total abjection and collapse, the last stanza, especially
the last line, outdoes all the rest. For the rhythm and
the images—the procession of hearses, the victor hoist-
ing a flag over the enemy's captured citadel—all these
are in the grand style; but the victor is Dread, of the
poet nothing remains, no soul, no brow, not even a
head; what has bowed down beneath the black flag is
only a skull, *mon crâne incliné.* He has lost all dignity,
not before God, for there is no God, but before Dread.

In our analysis we have tried to bring out two ideas,
both of which take the form of antitheses. First the
antithesis between symbolism and realism. Obviously
the poet's aim is not to give an accurate, realistic description of rain and a damp moldering dungeon, of

bats and spiders, the ringing of bells, and a bowed human skull. It makes no difference whether or not he ever actually heard bells ringing on a rainy day. The whole is a vision of despair, and the expository statements are purely symbolic. The data are of so little importance that the symbols can be changed without loss; Hope first appears as a bat, but the end, where she weeps in defeat, suggests the image of an infant or child, certainly not of a bat. Thus the poem cannot be called realistic if by realism we mean an attempt to reproduce outward reality. But since in the nineteenth century the word "realism" was associated chiefly with the crass representation of ugly, sordid, and horrifying aspects of life; since this was what constituted the novelty and significance of realism, the word was applicable to ugly, gruesome images, regardless of whether they were intended as concrete description or as symbolic metaphors. What mattered was the vividness of the evocation, and in this respect Baudelaire's poem is extremely realistic. Though the images evoked are wholly symbolic in intention, they forcefully concretize a hideous and terrible reality —even when reason tells us that such symbols can have no empirical reality. Obviously, there is no one by the name of Angoisse who can plant a black flag over a bowed skull: but the image of the *crâne incliné* is so overpowering that we see the gruesome portrait. The same is true of the spiders in the brain or the leaping, whimpering bells. These images strike with a realistic force that no one can escape; nor does the poet want anyone to escape them.

The other idea stressed in our analysis is the contradiction between the lofty tone and the indignity both of its subject as a whole and of many details. This contrast affected many contemporaries as an inconsistency of style; it was violently attacked at the time, though since then the "mixed style" has gained general acceptance. Modern critics, beginning in Baudelaire's time but more persistently in later years, have attempted to deny the hierarchy of literary objects, maintaining that there is no such things as sublime and base objects, but only good and bad verses, good and bad images. However, the formulation is misleading; it obscures the significant thing that happened in the nineteenth century movement. In classical aesthetics, subject matter and the manner of its treatment came to be divided into three classes: there was the great, tragic, and sublime; then the middle, pleasing, and inoffensive; finally the ridiculous, base, and grotesque. Within each of the three categories there were many gradations and special cases. A classification of this sort corresponds to human feeling, in Europe at least; it cannot be argued away. What the nineteenth century accomplished—and the twentieth has carried the process still further—was to change the basis of correlation: it became possible to take subjects seriously that had hitherto belonged to the low or middle category, and to treat them tragically. The subject matter of Flaubert or Cézanne, Zola or Van Gogh, is not "neutral"; one cannot say that their originality consisted solely in the novelty or perfection of their techniques; there can be no significant new technique without new content. The truth is rather that the subject matter became serious and great through the intention of those who gave it form. The same may be said of Baudelaire's *Fleurs du mal*. On February 28, 1866, he wrote to Ancelle: *Dans ce livre atroce, j'ai mis toute ma pensée, tout mon cœur, toute ma religion (travestie), toute ma haine. . .* (Into this abominable book I have put all my thought, all my religion [travestied], all my hatred). He could not have written in this way if he had not seen all human tragedy, depth, and greatness in his subject matter and intended to express them in his poems. It is futile to ask to what extent he posed and exaggerated; posture and exaggeration were an inherent part of the man and his state of mind. All modern artists (since Petrarch at least), have tended to dramatize themselves. The artistic process requires a concentration on certain themes, a process of selection, which stresses certain aspects of the artist's inner life and puts others aside. It was not easy for Baudelaire to live with himself and make himself work. He inclined to exaggerate his state and to make a display of what he rightly felt to be original and unique. But his concentration on certain themes that were distinctly his own and the force of his expression leave no room for doubt as to his fundamental authenticity.

He is authentic, and his conceptions are large; his poetry is in the grand style. But even among those whose intentions were similar, he is an extreme case; he is distinguished even from Rimbaud by his inner stagnation, his lack of development. He was the first to treat matters as sublime which seemed by nature unsuited to such treatment. The "spleen" of our poem is hopeless despair; it cannot be reduced to concrete causes or remedied in any way. A vulgarian would ridicule it; a moralist or a physician would suggest ways of curing it. But with Baudelaire their efforts would have been vain. He wrote in the grand style about paralyzing anxiety, panic at the hopeless entanglement of our lives, total collapse—a highly honorable undertaking, but also a negation of life. German slang has an apt term for this spleen: *das graue Elend,* the gray misery. Is the gray misery tragic? One should not be in too much of a hurry to dismiss as philistines the contemporary critics who rejected this form of poetry; what would Plato have thought of it? Baudelaire himself found a very similar term for his spleen, *ma triste misère*. It occurs in his poem *"Le Mauvais Moine";* after a half ironic picture of the medieval monks, who painted pictures of death and the truths of religion to console them for the ascetic austerity of their lives, he concludes as follows:

> *Mon âme est un tombeau que, mauvais cénobite,*
> *Depuis l'éternité je parcours et j'habite;*
> *Rien n'embellit les murs de ce cloître odieux.*
>
> *O moine fainéant! quand saurai-je donc faire*
> *Du spectacle vivant de ma triste misère*
> *Le travail de mes mains et l'amour de mes yeux?*

> (My soul is a tomb which, miserable monk,
> I have paced for all eternity. There I live
> In a hateful cloister to which nothing lends beauty.
>
> O idle monk! When shall I learn
> To turn the living vision of my bitter misery
> Into the work of my hands, the beloved of my eyes).

These verses present a new problem, though one implied in what has been said above. It is characteristic of the gray misery that it incapacitates one for all activity. Even those who cope with such depressions more successfully than Baudelaire, force themselves at best to carry on some routine activity; most of these are helped by their milieu or by an occupation that obliges them to do certain things at certain hours. In many cases this kind of activity has relieved or overcome the gray misery. But Baudelaire had no milieu or occupation requiring regular activity. Instead, he demanded of himself something far more difficult, something well-nigh impossible, and he succeeded: he managed to form his *triste misère* into poetry, to leap directly from his misery into the sublime, to fashion it into the work of his hands, the beloved of his eyes.

His passion for expressing himself drove him into an unremitting struggle with his gray misery, a battle in which he was sometimes victorious; not often, and never completely enough to cast it off; for strange to say, the gray misery was not merely the enemy, but also the beginning and object of his activity. What could be more paradoxical? The misery that paralyzed and degraded him was the source of a poetry that seems endowed with the highest dignity; it was the source both of the sublime tone produced by the fact of working under such desperate conditions and of the breaches of style that sprang directly from the subject matter.

The poet's misery had still other aspects, the most painful being his sexuality. Sexuality was a hell for him, a hell of degrading desire (*Lusthölle;* I believe that Thomas Mann uses the expression in *Doctor Faustus*). Here again we shall stick to the texts and begin with a poem without any concretely erotic content:

> *Je te donne ces vers afin que si mon nom*
> *Aborde heureusement aux époques lointaines,*
> *Et fait rêver un soir les cervelles humaines,*
> *Vaisseau favorisé par un grand aquilon,*
>
> *Ta mémoire, pareille aux fables incertaines,*
> *Fatigue le lecteur ainsi qu'un tympanon,*
> *Et par un fraternel et mystique chaînon*
> *Reste comme pendue à mes rimes hautaines;*
>
> *Etre maudit à qui, de l'abîme profond*
> *Jusqu'au plus haut du ciel, rien, hors moi, ne répond!*
> *—O toi qui, comme une ombre à la trace éphémère,*
>
> *Foules d'un pied léger et d'un regard serein*
> *Les stupides mortels qui t'ont jugée amère,*
> *Statue aux yeux de jais, grand ange au front d'airain!*

(I give you these verses, hoping that if my name,
Like a vessel favored by a stout north wind,
Should happily accost in epochs now remote
And stir a dream one night in human minds,

Your memory like a dubious fable
Will clang in the reader's ears and torment him,
Your memory suspended by an intimate
And mystic chain from my lofty rhymes;

Accursed one, whom from deepest depths to highest
Heights, no one will answer for but me!
You who like an ephemeral shadow

Pass light-footed and serene
Over the stupid mortals who have judged you vile,
Statue with eyes of jet, towering angel with head of
    brass.)

Syntactically, this poem too consists of a single sweeping movement: the simple and solemn main clause (*Je te donne ces vers*); dependent on it a long and intricate purpose clause, the subject of which appears only at the start of the second quatrain (*Ta mémoire*); followed, in the concluding tercets, by the apostrophe in three parts (*Etre maudit à qui . . . ; O toi qui . . . ; Statue . . .*). No less lofty seems the content: a poem is solemnly dedicated to the loved one, in order that she may, at some time in the distant future, partake of his fame. The reader is reminded of similar passages in which earlier poets, Horace, Dante, Petrarch, Ronsard, or Shakespeare (some critics have even mentioned Corneille and Byron) have spoken in lofty style of their future fame, sometimes in connection with a beloved. The words *je te donne ces vers*, with the ensuing image of a ship putting into port after a long voyage, seem quite consonant with this sublime tradition. And the singling out of a particular

moment (*un soir*) when the poet's fame will go into
effect, recalls a famous sonnet by Ronsard. But then
the reader, prepared for grandeur and dignity, is
shocked by the word *cervelles* (in the first version the
line read *Fit travailler un soir les cervelles humaines*);
the value of the poet's enduring fame becomes
strangely dubious. The reader dimly suspects what
becomes a certainty in the next stanza: the fame of
which the poet is going to speak will not enrich future
generations and gladden their hearts; it will irritate
and torment them (*ta mémoire . . . fatigue le lecteur
ainsi qu'un tympanon*), drawing the future reader into
a noxious entanglement. The distasteful memory of
the beloved to whom the poem is solemnly dedicated
will remain attached to the poet's proud verses *par un
fraternel et mystique chaînon*—in other words, the
memory is not proud or lofty, but base and unpleasant,
and it will be drummed into the reader's mind with
a perverse insistence. The whole poem is a piece of
bitter malice, not only against the beloved (we employ
the word only because no other is available), but also
against the future reader; for now, retroactively, the
afin que of the first line takes on an insidious meaning:
the poet's purpose in his *rimes hautaines* is malignant:
to tyrannize the future reader and avenge himself
against the beloved. In the final apostrophe the latter
theme is explicitly developed; for the apostrophe—in
three parts—is a curse; the beloved is described first
in relation to the poet, then in relation to the rest of
mankind, and finally for herself. Here we shall not
go into the separate themes—the poet at the mercy of
an outcast; her indifference; the mysterious presence
of this unmoving statue, this angel of evil. Yet in the
end something akin to admiration and adoration enters into the curse, expressed in a last haughty gibe,
this one at the *stupides mortels qui t'ont jugée amère.*

This poem, so rich in contradictions, sustains its lofty tone from the first to the last word. The curse ends with something in the nature of an apotheosis.

What all this means is known to us from other poems that deal directly with love or desire. Rhythm, form, and attitude place nearly all of them in the lofty style. But the traditional themes of sublime love poetry are almost wholly lacking; the accent is on naked sexuality, particularly in its terrible, abysmal aspects. If we are fully to understand the profound significance of Baudelaire we must recall the place of such things in the European literary tradition. Traditionally, physical love was treated in the light style.[2] In the older poetry the perverse or abject aspect is scarcely mentioned in any category of style.[3] In Baudelaire it is dominant. Traditional echoes are not wholly absent, such as the theme of the worshipped beloved (Muse, Madonna), but they ring false; sometimes they sound ironic and always strangely disfigured. The intimate tenderness that had gained a place beside the sublime in the love poetry of the early romantics also appears here and there in Baudelaire (*Mon enfant, ma sœur . . .*); but it is not the same idyllic intimacy as in the romantics, which would have been quite incompatible with Baudelaire's temperament; in him it has a new and strange aftertaste.

Almost everywhere in Baudelaire the relation between lovers—or more accurately between those bound by sexual attraction—is represented as an obsession mingled with hatred and contempt, an addiction which loses none of its degrading, tormenting force for being experienced in full (yet defenseless) awareness. Love is a torment, at best a numbing of the senses; true, it is also the source of inspiration, the actual source of the mystical intuition of the supernatural; nevertheless it is torture and degradation. Sometimes the loved one is sick and no longer young, more often she is a kind of bestial idol, soulless, barren, and morally indifferent. Baudelaire's masterly rendition of synesthetic impressions, in which the sense of smell is dominant (*respirer le parfum de ton sang; des parfums frais comme des chairs d'enfants; forêt aromatique* of the hair) helps to create a unique impression, at once sensuous, cold, bestial, painful, demonic, and sublime. All this is sufficiently known.

There seem to be isolated exceptions. Among the poems known or presumed to have been addressed to Madame Sabatier,[4] there are some in which health and untarnished beauty are praised; at first sight they seem to belong to a freer and happier order of poetry. But if we consider these poems in context, we soon begin to question our first impression. First of all we find that exuberant carnal health is strangely equated with sanctity and power to redeem. We begin to interpret the beautiful but very strange line *Sa chair spirituelle a le parfum des Anges* (from "*Que diras-tu ce soir . . .*") with the help of certain other lines, such as

> *Le passant chagrin que tu frôles*
> *Est ébloui par ta santé*
> *Qui jaillit comme une clarté*
> *De tes bras et de tes épaules,*
> ("*A celle qui est trop gaie*")

(The downcast passer-by
Is dazzled by your health
Which springs like a radiance
From your arms and your shoulders.)

or

> *David mourant aurait demandé la santé*
> *Aux émanations de ton corps enchanté*
>   ("*Réversibilité*")

(King David on his deathbed would have sought
Health in the aura of your enchanted flesh.)

There is something startling and incongruous about
this spiritualization and worship of so blatantly carnal
a magic (*L'Ange gardien, La Muse et la Madone,* or
Chère Déesse, Etre lucide et pur). And as a matter of
fact the picture is false. All this health and vitality is
intolerable to the poet; as we have said before, the
sunshine is of little use to him; hatred and lust for
destruction spring up side by side with admiration and
worship:

> *Folle dont je suis affolé,*
> *Je te hais autant que je t'aime!*
>
> *Quelquefois dans un beau jardin*
> *Où je traînais mon atonie,*
> *J'ai senti, comme une ironie,*
> *Le soleil déchirer mon sein;*
>
> *Et le printemps et la verdure*
> *Ont tant humilié mon cœur,*
> *Que j'ai puni sur une fleur*
> *L'insolence de la Nature.*

> (Madcap who maddens me
> I hate you as much as I love you!
>
> Sometimes in a bright garden
> Whither I dragged by atony,
>
> I have felt the sun like an irony
> Tearing my heart.
>
> And the spring with its verdure
> So humbled my heart
> That I punished Nature's insolence
> By trampling a flower.)

These lines[5] are from *"A celle qui est trop gaie,"*

one of the poems condemned by the court as immoral; it ends with an outburst of destructive frenzy (*Ainsi je voudrais, une nuit . . . pour châtier ta chair joyeuse . . . t'infuser mon venin, ma sœur!*).

The hatred and torment contained in these poems would have struck the taste of an earlier period as intolerable; no one would have looked at and treated the torments of love (and is one justified in speaking of love?) in this way; there is nothing comparable in the romantics, not at least in their poetry. Many poets since the Provençal troubadours have been prevented by their heavy hearts from enjoying the springtime. This may be called an almost traditional theme. One need only read Petrarch's 42nd Sonnet, *"In morte di Madonna Laura"* (*Zefiro torna*), to realize what a breach of style Baudelaire had committed.

One cannot but conclude that all those poems in *Les Fleurs du mal* which deal with erotic subjects are either filled with the harsh and painful disharmony that we have been trying to describe—or else are visions in which the poet strives to conjure up torpor, forgetfulness, the absolute Somewhere-Else.[6] Almost everywhere we find degradation and humiliation. The desirer becomes a slave, conscious but without will; the object of desire is without humanity and dignity, unfeeling, made cruel by her power and by ennui, barren, destructive; quotations and analyses are superfluous—all this is well-known to the readers of *Les Fleurs du mal*. Still, we should like to cite a few particularly glaring and magnificent examples of breach of style.[7] In the *"Hymne à la Beauté,"* we have the line:

> *Tu répands des parfums comme un soir orageux*
>
> (You scatter perfume like a stormy evening)

and a few lines further on the power of beauty is praised as follows:

> *Le Destin charmé suit tes jupons comme un chien*

> (Destiny spellbound follows your petticoats like a dog)

and this is how the lover looks to him:

> *L'amoureux pantelant incliné sur sa belle*
> *A l'air d'un moribond caressant son tombeau.*

> (The panting lover bending over his fair one
> Looks like a dying man caressing his grave.)

Among the portrayals of desire we have chosen two;
the reader is invited to savor their rhythm and content:

> *Je m'avance à l'attaque, et je grimpe aux assauts,*
> *Comme après un cadavre un chœur de vermisseaux*
> *("Je t'adore")*

> (I spring to the attack, I mount to the assault
> Like a chorus of maggots besetting a corpse)

and

> *Je frissonne de peur quand tu me dis: "Mon ange!"*
> *Et cependant je sens ma bouche aller vers toi.*[8]
> *("Femmes damnées")*

> (I tremble with fear when you say: "My angel!"
> And yet my lips move toward you.)

Now the degradation of the flesh, and particularly
the equations of woman-sin and desire-death-putrefac-
tion belong to a Christian tradition that was particularly strong toward the end of the Middle Ages. It
was inevitable that certain critics should have related
Baudelaire to this tradition, especially since he was
sharply opposed to the tendencies of the Enlighten-
ment and since prayers or something very close to it
already make their appearance in *Les Fleurs du mal*.
It is certainly true that like the romantics before him,
he was influenced by Christian-medieval images and

ideas. It is also true that Baudelaire had the mind of a mystic; in the world of the senses he looked for the supernatural, and found a second sensory world that was supernatural, demonic, and hostile to nature. Finally it may be said—and indeed it has been said— that the view of sensory reality that we find in *Les Fleurs du mal* would have been inconceivable in the pagan world. But that is as far as one may go. We owe it to the Christian tradition to point out that although the central trend of *Les Fleurs du mal* would have been unthinkable without the Christian tradition, it is fundamentally different from the Christian tradition, and incompatible with it. Here we shall sum up the essential points of difference:

1. What the poet of *Les Fleurs du mal* is looking for is not grace and eternal beatitude but either nothingness, *le Néant*,[9] or a kind of sensory fulfillment, the vision of a sterile, but sensuous artificiality (*volupté calme; ordre et beauté; luxe, calme et volupté;* cf. also the vision contained in "*Rêve parisien*"). His spiritualization of memory and his synesthetic symbolism are also sensory, and behind them stands not any hope of redemption through God's grace, but nothingness, the absolute Somewhere-Else.

2. In any Christian interpretation of life, redemption by the Incarnation and Passion of Christ is the cardinal point of universal history and the source of all hope. There is no place for Christ in *Les Fleurs du mal*. He appears but once, in "*Le Reniement de Saint-Pierre*," and here he is at odds with God. This notion occurs earlier in some of the romantics; but to the mind of a believer no greater confusion or error is conceivable. Even from a historical point of view it is a dilettantish misunderstanding of the Christian tradition. This second point is not basically different from

the first, but complements it and gives a still clearer picture of Baudelaire's situation.

3. The corruption of the flesh means something very different in *Les Fleurs du mal* and in the Christianity of the late Middle Ages. In *Les Fleurs du mal* the desire that is damned is most often a desire for the physically corrupt or misshapen; the enjoyment of young, healthy flesh is never held up as a sin. In the warnings and castigations of the Christian moralists, on the other hand, the object of carnal temptation may have been represented as the creature of an hour, but for the present she was endowed with youth and full-blown earthly health. There was nothing decrepit about Eve with the apple; her apparent soundness is what made the temptation so insidious, and in Christian morality it is condemned. The poet of *Les Fleurs du mal* knows youth, vitality, health, only as objects of yearning and admiration—or else of malignant envy. Sometimes he wants to destroy them, but in the main he tends to spiritualize, admire, and worship them.[10]

4. In *Les Fleurs du mal,* Baudelaire is not striving for humility, but for pride. To be sure, he degrades himself and all earthly life, but in the midst of his degradation he does his best to sustain his pride. In this connection we might mention the lines of prayer in *"Bénédiction" (Soyez béni, mon Dieu, qui donnez la souffrance . . .).* They are very moving, but the idea that fills them is that of the poet's own apotheosis; singling himself out from the contemptible race of men, he appears before the face of God. Such verses could scarcely have been written before Rousseau's famous apostrophe to God at the beginning of the *Confessions.* Neither writer is innocent of self-aggrandizement.[11]

What I am saying here refers solely to *Les Fleurs du mal*. We have no wish to speak of the salvation of Baudelaire's soul, and it would be beyond our means to do so. It is easy to understand that important Catholic critics should have concerned themselves not only with Baudelaire but also with other desperate rebels of the nineteenth century, and attempted to interpret them as exemplary vehicles of the struggle for faith and witnesses to the triumph of Grace. Souls such as Baudelaire's are the *âmes choisies* of our time or at least of a time that is not too far in the past.[12] But that is not our concern; we are speaking not of the history of Baudelaire's soul but of *Les Fleurs du mal*. It is a work of despair and of the bitter pleasures of despair. Its world is a prison; sometimes the pain is deadened or appeased, and sometimes, too, there is the ecstatic pleasure of artistic self-exaltation; but escape from the prison there is none. Nor can there be. Jean-Paul Sartre, an acute and concrete thinker though his designs obtrude too much, has shown brilliantly[13] how Baudelaire the man consciously ran himself into a dead end and how he himself blocked off every exit or retreat. In order to determine the historical position of *Les Fleurs du mal,* it is important to observe that in the middle of the nineteenth century a man was able to fashion this character and this biography and that this kind of man was able to achieve full expression at just this time, so that he disclosed something that was latent in his age, which many men gradually came to perceive through him. The periods of human history prepare their prospective representatives; they seek them out, shape them, bring them to light, and through them make themselves known.

There is no way out, nor can there be. The poet of *Les Fleurs du mal* hated the reality of the time in which he lived; he despised its trends, progress and prosperity, freedom and equality; he recoiled from its pleasures; he hated the living, surging forces of nature;[14] he hated love insofar as it is "natural." And his contempt for all these things was only increased by his awareness that he had never experienced or ventured seriously to approach a good many of them. He invoked the forces of faith and transcendence only insofar as they could be used as weapons against life, or as symbols of escape; or insofar as they could serve his jealous, exclusive worship of what he really loved and pursued with all the strength that was left him after so much hopeless resistance: absolute poetic creation, absolute artifice, and himself as the artificial creator. Here it is worth our while to take up a text, *"La Mort des artistes,"* the poem with which he concluded the first edition of *Les Fleurs du mal.* In its final form (1861)[15] it runs as follows:

> *Combien faut-il de fois secouer mes grelots*
> *Et baiser ton front bas, morne caricature?*
> *Pour piquer dans le but, de mystique nature,*
> *Combien, ô mon carquois, perdre de javelots?*
>
> *Nous userons notre âme en de subtils complots,*
> *Et nous démolirons mainte lourde armature,*
> *Avant de contempler la grande Créature*
> *Dont l'infernal désir nous remplit de sanglots!*
>
> *Il en est qui jamais n'ont connu leur Idole,*
> *Et ces sculpteurs damnés et marqués d'un affront,*
> *Qui vont se martelant la poitrine et le front,*
>
> *N'ont qu'un espoir, étrange et sombre Capitole!*
> *C'est que la Mort, planant comme un soleil nouveau,*
> *Fera s'épanouir les fleurs de leur cerveau!*

(How many times more shall I have to shake my bells
And kiss your low forehead, dismal caricature?

Before I hit the mystic target
How many arrows shall I lose from my quiver?

We shall waste our souls in subtle schemes,
And shatter many a heavy armature
Before we behold the great Creature
Who has damned us to heartbreaking desire.

There are some who have never known their idol,
And these accursed sculptors marked by an affront,
Who chisel out their own chests and foreheads,

Have but one hope, o strange and somber Capitol!
It is that Death, soaring like a new sun
Will bring the flowers of their brain to blossoming.)

There can be little doubt that he is speaking of the artist's struggle for something absolute; a striving, warped by bitter hopelessness, for the idea or archetype in the Platonic or Neoplatonic sense. The *morne caricature,* before which the artist humiliates himself like a clown, can be nothing other than the debased earthly appearance; the poet expends his powers trying to pass through it to the mystic archetype. Thus far the poem, despite the extreme sharpness with which it expresses the indignity of the earthly appearance, is still compatible with the traditional idea of an ascent to the vision of the archetype. But what is quite incompatible with this long tradition is the way in which Baudelaire speaks of the archetype itself. First it is called *la grande Créature,* which has a sensual, pejorative ring, and which in readers familiar with *Les Fleurs du mal* evokes demonic insensibility and sterile lust for power (cf. *"Hymne à la Beauté," "La Beauté"*); and a little later, with evident scorn, he calls it *leur Idole.* Still more shocking is what he says of the striving for the archetype. In the whole of mystical and visionary literature this striving, however arduous and vain, was never represented as anything other than great and noble; it was held to be the highest form of endeavor and activity that a man could elect. But the author of our verses calls it *infernal désir,* as though it were a vice. The methods it employs are *subtils complots,* which wear out the soul. Those who never get to see their *idole* are accursed and degraded *(damnés et marqués d'un affront).* In the twentieth essay of his first book, Montaigne says: *L'entreprise se sent de la qualité de la chose qu'elle regarde; car c'est une bonne partie de l'effect, et consubstantielle.* ("The undertaking smacks of the quality of what it has in view; for the striving is a good part of the result, and consubstantial with it.") If this is true, and it is true, the degradation of the striving will degrade the goal. At the end of the poem, to be sure, there is a sudden rise; a hope seems to appear; its name is Death, *planant comme un soleil nouveau,* and it will "bring the flowers of their brain to blossoming." This again might fit in with the tradition. Beyond the vision which is sometimes granted a living man in *excessus mentis,* stands the sight of God in his glory, and this can never be taken away from the soul that has been saved. But here, in Baudelaire's poem, death is not eternal beatitude; this is made clear by the words *étrange et sombre Capitole,* which also exclude any other form of pure fulfillment in transcendence; there is a raucous note, a veiled mockery in the whole tercet whose rhythm seems to mount so abruptly. But what then of the hope? How can nothingness be a new sun that will bring flowers to unfolding? I know no answer. There is none to be found in *Les Fleurs du mal.*[16] Instead we find, immediately after our poem, a description of death in *"Le Rêve d'un curieux";* it ends with the following words:

J'étais mort sans surprise, et la terrible aurore
M'enveloppait. —Eh quoi! n'est-ce donc que cela?
La toile était levée et j'attendais encore.

(I had died unawares, and the terrible dawn
Enveloped me. —What, is it only this?
The curtain had risen, and still I was waiting.)

The archetype, *la grande Créature,* is for the poet
an object of desperate desire and at the same time of
contemptuous mockery. As transcendent reality it is
nothing, or worse than nothing: a nothing which by
its nothingness mocks and humiliates those who strive
for it.

But here he is unjust to himself. It is his unswerving
despair which gave him the dignity and weight that
he has for us. The unswerving honesty that made it
impossible for him to worship the Baalim for even one
moment in a time without gods, is his greatness. His
dandyism and his poses were merely a deformation imposed by the desperate struggle. Anyone who reads
him feels after the very first lines that his aesthetic
dandyism has nothing in common with the pre-Parnas-
sian and Parnassian aesthetes, with Gautier or Leconte
de Lisle. Baudelaire's poetry has a much wider range.
And he cannot hide himself behind his work. Degraded, deformed, and sublime, he is right in the middle of it. It is a book consubstantial with its author,
to cite Montaigne again. Paradigmatic for the whole
age, it gave this age a new poetic style: a mixture of
the base and contemptible with the sublime, a symbolic use of realistic horror, which was unprecedented
in lyric poetry and had never been carried to such
lengths in any genre. In him for the first time we find
fully developed those surprising and seemingly inco-
herent combinations that Royère calls *catachrèses,* and
which led Brunetière to accredit Baudelaire with the

génie de l'impropriété. We have quoted a few of them in the course of this study. *Des cloches tout à coup sautent avec furie, La Mort, planant comme un soleil nouveau,* etc. The visionary power of such combinations exerted a crucial influence on later poetry; they seemed the most authentic expression both of the inner anarchy of the age and of a still hidden order that was just beginning to dawn. In an entirely new and consummate style, this poet, whose character and life were so strange, expressed the naked, concrete existence of an epoch. For his style was not based on his personal situation and his personal needs; it became apparent that his extreme personality embodied a far more universal situation and a far more universal need. Now that the crisis of our civilizations (which at Baudelaire's time was still latent, presaged by only a few)—now that the crisis is approaching a decision, we may perhaps expect a decline in Baudelaire's influence; in a totally changed world that is perhaps moving toward a new order, the coming generations may lose contact with his problems and his attitude.[17] But the historic importance of *Les Fleurs du mal* can never be shaken. The human structure that appears in these poems is just as significant for the transformation, or perhaps one should say the destruction, of the European tradition as the human structure of Ivan Karamazov. The form, not only of modern poetry but also of the other literary genres of the century that has elapsed since then, is scarcely thinkable without *Les Fleurs du mal;* the trace of Baudelaire's influence can be followed in Gide, Proust, Joyce, and Thomas Mann as well as Rimbaud, Mallarmé, Rilke, and Eliot. Baudelaire's style, the mixture we have attempted to describe, is as much alive as ever.

And yet I do not wish this paper to end with the praise of Baudelaire's literary achievement, but rather on the note with which it began, the horror of *Les Fleurs du mal*. It is a book of gruesome hopelessness, of futile and absurd attempts to escape by inebriation and narcosis. Accordingly, a word should be said in defense of certain critics who have resolutely rejected the book. Not all of them, but a few, had a better understanding of it than many contemporary and subsequent admirers. A statement of horror is better understood by those who feel the horror in their bones, even if they react against it, than by those who express nothing but their rapture over the artistic achievement. Those who are seized with horror do not speak about *frisson nouveau;* they do not cry bravo and congratulate the poet on his originality. Even Flaubert's admiration, though excellently formulated, is too aesthetic.[18] Most later critics took it for granted that the book could only be considered from an aesthetic standpoint and scornfully rejected any other possibility from the outset. It seems to us that aesthetic criticism alone is unequal to the task, though Baudelaire would scarcely have shared our opinion: he was contaminated by the idolatry of art that is still with us. What a strange phenomenon: a prophet of doom who expects nothing of his readers but admiration for his artistic achievement. *Ponete mente almen com' io son bella* ("consider at least how beautiful I am")—with these words Dante concludes his *canzone* to the movers of the third heaven. But can such words be applied to poems whose meaning is so actual and urgent, whose beauty is as bitter as that of *Les Fleurs du mal?*

NOTES

NOTES

"Figura"

[1] As P. Friedlaender informs me, the *barbarica pestis* is probably the sting of a ray, by which Odysseus was mortally wounded; *subinis* is uncertain. [As is my translation of it. TRANS.]

[2] In late antiquity (Chalcidius, Isidore) and in the Middle Ages it reappears in a play on words with *pictura*. Cf. E. R. Curtius in *Zeitschrift für romanische Philologie*, 58 (1938), 45.

[3] Many later definitions take this direction. Cf. *Thesaurus Linguae Latinae*, VI, part 1, col. 722, 1. 54.

[4] In Aristotle (and in Plato) *typōi* means "in general," "in broad outlines," "as a rule." His phrase *pachulōs kai typōi* (*Nichomachean Ethics*, 1094b, 20), or *kath' holou lechthen kai typōi* was handed down by way of Irenaeus (2, 76) and Boethius (*Topicorum Aristoteles interpretatio*, 1, 1 [*Patrologia Latina*, LXIV, col. 911]) to the French and Italian, cf. Godefroy, s.v. *figural: Il convient que la manière de procéder en ceste œuvre soit grosse et figurele*. Or s.v. *figuralment: Car la manière de produyre/ Ne se peut monstrer ne deduyre/ Par effect, si non seulement/ Grossement et figuraulment* (Greban). In Italian the understanding for the combination *sommariamente e figuralmente* seems to have been lost at an early date; cf. the examples in Tommaseo-Bellini, *Dizionario della Lingua Italiana* (1869), II, part 1, p. 789, s.v. *figura* 18.

[5] *Schēma* has meanings that do not occur or that did not persist in *figura*, as, for example, the meaning of "constitution."

[6] Cf. also the shaping of tones in 2, 412-13: *per chordas orga-*

nici quae/ mobilibus digitis expergefacta figurant ("which harpers with nimble fingers arouse and shape on the strings").

[7] Accordingly, *forma* usually appears where two syllables are needed. Even in Lucretius the relation between the two words is rather loose and vacillating. There are passages, however, particularly in Lucretius, where the two concepts are sharply distinguished; as when he speaks of the primal elements:

> *quare . . . necessest*
> *natura quoniam constant neque facta manu sunt*
> *unius ad certam formam primordia rerum*
> *dissimili inter se quadam volitare figura.*
>
> (2, 377-80)

> (And so it must be that the first beginning of things, existing as they do by nature and not being hand-made after the definite form of one single pattern, must some of them have different shapes as they fly about.)

Like the *formai servare figuram* of 4, 69, this clearly expresses the well-known relation between *morphē* and *schēma*, which Ernout-Meillet, loc. cit. suggests with *la configuration du moule*. Cf. Cicero, *De natura deorum*, I, 90.

[8] The last three words (as Munro has pointed out) reflect the formula of Democritus and Leucippus: *rysmos, tropē, diathigē* (Cf. Diels, *Fragmente der Vorsokratiker*, 2, 4th edition, p. 22). Aristotle employs *schēma* in explaining *rysmos* (*Metaphysics*, 985b, 16 and 1042b, 11; *Physics*, 188a, 24). Lucretius translated the term by *figura*.

[9] A few passages: 2, 385, 514, 679, 682; 3, 190, 246; 6, 770.

[10] The transition from "*figura* of the material" to "*figura* of the reproduced object" was effected only very gradually, first in the poets. Cf. (aside from Lucretius) Catullus, 64, 50, and 64, 265; Propertius, 2, 6, 33. In Velleius Paterculus, 1, 11, 4, *Expressa similitudine figurarum* means "portraitlike."

[11] Cf. also *Ad familiares*, 15, 16. On the other hand, Quintilian, 10, 2, 15: *illas Epicuri figuras . . .* ("those *figurae* of Epicurus").

[12] Later *figura* becomes quite frequent in the sense of "divine image"—and, in the Christian authors, of "idol"—or of the image on a coin.

[13] In Propertius and also in Ovid, *figurae* ("forms") at times

means "kind," "manner," as opposed to "class," "sort"; this is the same evolution as *species-espèce*.

[14] In connection with pastry, cf. also Martial, 14, 222, 1; Festus, 129, *ficta quaedam ex farina in hominum figuras* ("things made of dough in the shapes of men"); and Petronius, 33, 6, *ova ex farina figurata* ("eggs fashioned of meal"). The pastry-cook was often regarded and employed as a sculptor and decorator, an attitude revived by later periods, particularly the Renaissance, and the baroque and rococo periods; Cf. Goethe, *Wilhelm Meister's Lehrjahre,* Book 3, Chapter 7, and Creizenach's note on this passage in the Jubiläumsausgabe, Vol. 17, p. 344.

[15] In *Epist.,* 65, 7, Seneca has a passage significant in another connection, where *figura* stands for archetype, idea, *forma,* but in the Neoplatonic sense of the inner model of the forms in the mind of the artist. In this passage he also makes the comparison, which later became so frequent, between the artist and the Creator: the sculptor, says Seneca, can find the model (*exemplar*) of his work in himself or outside; it can be provided him by his eyes or his mind; and God has within him all the *exemplaria* of things: *plenus his figuris est quas Plato ideas appellat immortales* ("He is full of those figures that Plato calls immortal ideas"). Cf. Dürer: "For a good painter is inwardly full of figures (*voller Figur*); cf. E. Panofsky, *Idea* (1924), p. 70.

[16] See Faral, *Les Arts poétiques du 12ème et du 13ème siècle* (Paris, 1924), pp. 48 ff. and 99 ff.

[17] A noteworthy variant occurs in Ammianus Marcellinus, who uses the word for the topography of battlefields. Cf. *Thesaurus Linguae Latinae,* VI, part 1, 726, 37 ff.

[18] In Sedulius, *Carmen Paschale,* 5, 101-2, there is a passage in which *figura* can hardly mean anything other than "face," as in modern French:

> *Namque per hos colaphos caput est sanabile nostrum;*
> *Haec sputa per Dominum nostram lavere figuram.*

> (For our head can be healed by these blows. This spittle has washed our face in the Lord's person.)

Since the poet had spoken previously of *spuere in faciem* ("spitting in the face") and *colaphis pulsare caput* ("plying the head with blows"), the meaning of "face" cannot be doubted;

still, it is possible that Sedulius was led to choose the more general *figura* by the need for a trisyllable with a long middle syllable with which to conclude the line. In any event it is the only certain ancient example known to us of Latin *figura* for "face." Jeanneret's presumption, in *La Langue des tablettes d'exécration latines* (Neuchâtel, 1918), p. 108, that *figura* in the Minturnian tablet of execration means "face," is certainly unfounded, if only because of the juxtaposition with *membra* and *colorem*, which is very frequent. In the sense of "form" it belongs to the general attributes (or parts) of the body, with which the curse begins: then follow the special attributes. Jeanneret's contention is also rejected by Wartburg in FEW, *ad v. figura,* 9. The question remains unsettled in regard to a fragment of Laberius: *figura humana inimico (nimio) ardore ignescitur,* Ribbeck, 2, p. 343.

[19] In the Septuagint Joshua is already called Jesus, which is a contraction of Joshua. Cf. the illustrations of the Vatican Scroll of Joshua, which is thought to be a sixth-century copy of a fourth-century original. The only part of it now available to me is a page in K. Pfister's *Mittelalterlicher Buchmalerei* (Munich, 1922), representing the setting up of the twelve stones (Josh. 4:20-1); in text and inscription Joshua is called *Iēsous ho tou Nauē* ("Jesus [the son] of Nave"), bears a halo, and is plainly intended to suggest Christ. Later allusions to the "figure" of Joshua are frequent; cf. Hildebert of Tours, *Sermones de diversis,* XXIII, *Patrologia Latina,* Vol. 171, cols. 842 ff.

[20] *Figuraretur* means here at once "would be formed" and "would be figured," the latter by blood and water, the Lord's Supper and baptism. The juxtaposition of the two wounds in the side long remained an important theme. Cf. Burdach, *Vorspiel,* I, 1 (1925), pp. 162 and 212; Dante, *Par.,* 13, 37 ff.

[21] *Ita et nunc sanguinem suum in vino consecravit qui tunc vinum in sanguine figuravit* ("so now also he consecrated his blood in wine who then had figured wine in blood").

[22] Moses is in general a figuration of Christ, e.g., in the crossing of the Red Sea or the transformation of the bitter water into sweet water for baptism. But this does not prevent him, in the first example, from figuring the law in contradiction to his figuration of Christ.

²³ Cf. Hilary of Poitiers, *Tractatus mysteriorum,* 1 *(Corp. Vind.,* Vol. 65, p. 3), quoted in Labriolle, *History and Literature of Christianity* (London and New York, 1924), p. 243.

²⁴ Cf. Hilarian, *De cursu temporum, Patrologia Latina,* 13, col. 173, 2: *sabbati aeterni imaginem et figuram tenet sabbatus temporalis* ("the temporal sabbath is an image and figure of the eternal sabbath").

²⁵ How deeply ingrained the habit of interpretation had become in this world may be seen from the half jesting interpretation of gifts in the correspondence of St. Jerome (Letter 44, *Selected Letters of St. Jerome,* M. F. A. Wright [London and New York, 1933], pp. 176-7).

²⁶ St. Jerome attacks Origen for this, saying that he is *allegoricus semper interpres et historiae fugiens veritatem . . . nos simplicem et veram sequamur historiam ne quibusdam nubibus atque praestigiis involvamur* (Jeremiam 27, 3, 4; *Patrologia Latina,* 24, col. 849) ("always an allegorical exegete, shunning historical truth . . . as for us, let us simply follow the true history and not involve ourselves in phantasms and charlatanism"). On the relation of the Alexandrians, particularly Origen, to figural interpretation, cf. A. Freiherr von Ungern-Sternberg, *Der traditionelle Alttestamentl. Schriftbeweis . . .* (Halle, 1913), pp. 154 ff. On p. 160 he says of Origen: "He did not live in the biblical realism of scriptural proof."

²⁷ Cf. also *De civ.,* 15, 27; ibid., 20, 21 *(Ad Isaiam,* 65, 17ff.).

²⁸ A. Rüstow calls my attention to the following stanza in a Shrovetide play by Hans Folz (about 1500):

> *Hör Jud, so merk dir und verstee*
> *Dass alle Geschicht der alten Ee*
> *Und aller Propheten Red gemein*
> *Ein Figur der neuen Ee ist allein.*

(Hear, Jew, take note and understand that the whole history of the old covenant and all the sayings of the Prophets are only a figure for the new covenant.)

²⁹ *Corp. Vind.,* Vol. 31, cf. Labriolle, op. cit., p. 424.

³⁰ In addition, of course, we find *claudere* ("to close, conceal"), in recollection of Isa. 22:22 and Rev. 3:7. Cf. at a later day Peter Lombard, *Commentarium in Ps.,* 146, 6 *(Patrologia*

Latina, Vol. 191, col. 1276): *clausa Dei* "what God has concealed by obscurity of expression," and *prov. clus.*

[31] Quoted according to *Patrologia Latina,* 59, col. 360.

[32] Cf. Du Cange and Dante, *Purg.,* 10, 73, and 12, 22; Alain de Lille, *De planctu naturae, Patrologia Latina,* 210, 438; many passages might be found. Amyot says in *Thém.,* 52: *La parole de l'homme ressemble proprement à une tapisserie historiée et figurée* ("the speech of man truly resembles a figured and storied tapestry").

[33] Suggestions of figural prophecy are not entirely lacking in the Synoptic Gospels; as for example when Jesus likens himself to Jonah, Matt. 12:39 ff., Luke 11:29 ff. In St. John one might mention 5:46. But next to the passages in the Epistles, these are no more than feeble intimations.

[34] This was pointed out to me by R. Bultmann; the specialized literature is not available to me at the moment. Cf. among other passages Deut. 18:15; John 1:45; 6:14; 6:26 ff.; Acts 3:22 f.

[35] Sedulius, *Eleg.,* 1, 87: *Pellitur umbra die, Christo veniente figura* ("The shadow is dispelled by the day, the figure by Christ's coming").

[36] Though Prudentius does not seem to recognize figural interpretation, examples of it occur in his *Dittochaeon* (see Prudentius, ed. H. J. Thomson, 2 vols. [London and Cambridge (Mass.), 1949-53], Vol. 2, pp. 346 ff.).

[37] This includes legendary and mythical as well as strictly historical events. Whether the material to be interpreted is really historical or only passes as such is immaterial for our purpose.

[38] Cf. Emile Bréhier, *Les idées philosophiques de Philon d'Alexandrie,* 2d. ed. (Paris, 1925), pp. 35 ff.

[39] There are many intermediate forms combining figure and symbol; above all the Eucharist in which Christ is felt to be concretely present, and the cross as tree of life, *arbor vitae crucifixae,* which played a significant role extending roughly from the fourth-century poem *"De cruce,"* cf. Labriolle, op. cit., p. 318, to the "spiritual" Franciscan Ubertino de Casale or Dante and beyond.

[40] In the prayer corresponding to the *Quam oblationem* of the present-day Roman mass, the book *De sacramentis* (fourth cen-

tury) has the following text: *Fac nobis hanc oblationem ascrip-tam, ratam, rationabilem, acceptabilem, quod figura est corporis et sanguinis Christi. Qui pridie . . .* ("Make for us this offering consecrated, approved, reasonable, and acceptable, which is a figure of the body and blood of Christ. Who on the day before he suffered . . ."). See Dom F. Cabrol in *Liturgia: Encyclopédie populaire des connaissances liturgiques,* ed. R. Aigrain (Paris, 1930), p. 543. Cf. also a much later text, the *Rhythmus ad Sanctam Eucharistiam* (thirteenth century):

> *Adoro te devote, latens deitas*
> *Quae sub his figuris vere latitas*

> (Humbly I adore thee, hidden Deity
> which beneath these figures art concealed from me)

and later:

> *Jesu quem velatum nunc adspicio,*
> *Oro fiat illud quod tam sitio,*
> *Ut te revelata cernens facie*
> *Visu sim beatus tuae gloriae.*

> (Jesus whom thus veiled I must see below,
> When shall that be given which I long for so,
> That at last beholding thy uncovered face,
> Thou shalt satisfy me with thy fullest grace?)
> (Trans. J. M. Neale, *Collected Hymns*
> [London, 1914], p. 63.)

[41] Many allusions may be found in Gilson, *Les idées et les lettres,* esp. pp. 68 ff. and 155 ff. In his article, *"Le moyen âge et l'histoire"* (in *L'Esprit de la philosophie médiévale,* Paris, 1932) he refers to the figural element in the medieval philosophy of history, but with no great emphasis, since his main concern was to uncover the medieval roots of modern conceptions. Cf. also, for the German religious drama, T. Weber, *Die Praefigurationen in geistlichen Drama Deutschlands,* Marburg Dissertation 1909, and L. Wolff, *"Die Verschmelzung des Dargestellten mit der Gegenwartswirklichkeit im deutschen geistlichen Drama des Mittelalters," Deutsche Vierteljahrsschrift für Literaturwissenschaft und Geistesgeschichte,* 7, p. 267 ff. On figural

elements in the portrayal of Charlemagne in the *Chanson de Roland,* cf. A. Pauphilet's well-known article in *Romania,* LIX, esp. pp. 183 ff.

[42] Of course there are numerous analyses of the fourfold meaning of Scripture, but they do not bring out what strikes me as indispensable. It is natural that medieval theology, while distinctly differentiating the various forms of allegory (e.g., Petrus Comestor in the prologue to his *Historia scholastica*), should attribute no fundamental importance, but only a kind of technical interest to these distinctions. But even so outstanding a modern theologian as the Dominican Père Mandonnet, who gives an outline of the history of symbolism in his *Dante le Théologien* (Paris, 1935, pp. 163 ff.), regards the knowledge of these differentiations as a mere technical instrument for the understanding of texts, and takes no account of the different conceptions of reality involved.

[43] By that time of course the foundations of figural interpretation had already been destroyed; even many ecclesiastics no longer understood it. As Emile Mâle tells us (*L'Art religieux du 12ème siècle en France,* 3d ed., 1928, p. 391) Montfaucon interpreted the rows of Old Testament figures at the sides of certain church porches as Merovingian kings. In a letter from Leibniz to Burnett (1696, Gerhardt edition, III, 306) we find the following: "M. Mercurius van Helmont believed that the soul of Jesus Christ was that of Adam and that the new Adam repairing what the first had ruined was the same personage paying his old debt. I think one does well to spare oneself the trouble of refuting such ideas."

[44] In speaking of the architect, St. Thomas says *quasi idea* (*Quodlibetales,* IV, 1, 1). Cf. Panofsky, *Idea* (Leipzig, 1924), p. 20 ff. and note, p. 85; cf. also the quotation from Seneca in our note 15.

[45] See Zingarelli, *Dante,* 3d ed., 1931, pp. 1029 ff., and the literature cited in the note.

[46] Cf. J. Balogh in *Deutsches Dante-Jahrbuch,* 10, 1928, p. 202.

[47] Accordingly Dante, *Purg.,* 32, 102, describes *quelle Roma onde Cristo è Romano* ("that Rome whereof Christ is a Roman") as the fulfilled kingdom of God.

[48] *Purg.,* 22, 69-73, Temple Classics ed. The fact that in the

Middle Ages Virgil often appears among the prophets of Christ has been several times discussed in detail since Comparetti. A certain amount of new material is to be found in the festival volume, *Virgilio nel medio evo,* of the *Studi medievali* (N.S.V., 1932); I should like to make special mention of K. Strecker's *Iam nova progenies caelo dimittitur alto,* p. 167, where a bibliography and some material on figural structure in general may be found; further E. Mâle, *Virgile dans l'art du moyen âge,* p. 325, particularly plate 1; and Luigi Suttina, *L'effigie di Virgilio nella Cattedrale di Zamorra,* p. 342.

[49] The words *mi converrebbe essere laudatore di me medesimo* ("it would behove me to be a praiser of myself"), *Vita Nova,* (Temple Classics ed., p. 109) 29, are an allusion to II Cor. 12:1. Cf. Grandgent in *Romania,* 31, 14, and Scherillo's commentary.

[50] This is indicated by the title of the book, by his first designation of her as *la gloriosa donna de la mia mente* ("the glorious lady of my mind"), by the name-mysticism, the trinitarian significance of the number nine, by the effects emanating from her, etc., etc. Sometimes she appears as a *figura Christi;* one need only consider the interpretation of her appearance behind Monna Vanna (24); the events accompanying the vision of her death (23); eclipse, earthquake, the hosannas of the angels; and the effect of her appearance in *Purg.,* 30. Cf. Galahad in the *"Queste del Saint Graal,"* Gilson, *Les idées et les lettres,* p. 71.

[51] To avoid misunderstandings it should be mentioned here that Dante and his contemporaries termed the figural meaning "allegory," while they referred to what is here called allegory as "ethical" or "tropological" meaning. The reader will surely understand why in this historical study we have stuck to the terminology created and favored by the Church Fathers.

[52] He denies that she ever smiles in spite of *Purg.,* 31, 133 ff., and 32, beginning. His remarks on Beatrice may be found in op. cit., pp. 212 ff.

St. Francis of Assisi in Dante's "Commedia"

[1] Modern edition by P. Eduardus Alenconiensis in the *Analecta Ord. Min. Cap.* (1900).

[2] The writings of Fr. Dölger dealing with this subject are unfortunately inaccessible to me. Cf. the *Commentary* of Pietro Alighieri (Florence, 1845), pp. 626 ff., which quotes Gregory the Great on Job 1:3.

[3] Is it perhaps a feeling for paradox painful to good taste that has led many copyists and editors to write *pianse* for *salse* or at least to prefer this reading? It seems to me wrong, for it blunts the contrast between Maria and Paupertas. The *Testo Critico* has *pianse,* the Oxford edition *salse.* The only old manuscript at my disposal, the famous Frankfurt ms. in the reproduction of the German Dante Society, certainly has *pianse.*

[4] *Franzisce, nimm die bitteren Ding für die süssen und verschmäh dich selber, dass du mich bekennen magst.* Quoted from the collection of Severin Rüttgers, *Der Heiligen Leben und Leiden* (Leipzig, 1922). The passage is based on a sentence from the saint's testament: *Et recedente me ab ipsis* [the lepers], *id quod videbatur michi amarum, conversum fuit michi in dulcedinum animi et corporis. Analekten zur Geschichte des Franciscus v. A.,* ed. H. Boehmer (Tübingen and Leipzig, 1940), p. 36.

[5] See pp. 11-76 in this volume. [TRANS.]

On the Political Theory of Pascal

[1] The subject of this essay has been treated by Jacques Maritain, "The Political Ideas of Pascal," in *Ransoming the Time* (New York, 1941), pp. 33 ff., and Romano Guardini in *Christliches Bewustsein* (Leipzig, 1935), pp. 139 ff.

[2] There is no contradiction between this and the fact that Port-Royal was in many ways involved in the political movements and problems of the time.

[3] Actually these *Discours* were first committed to writing by Nicole, after Pascal's death and ten years after they were delivered. However, they are perfectly in the spirit of the *Pensées,* in which we find the same ideas.

[4] A good practical example may be found in a document dating from the war of investitures: "*Leodicensium epistula ad Pascalem papam,*" in the *Libelli de Lite* (*Mon. Germaniae Hist.,* Vol. II, p. 461). Cf. G. Tellenbach, *Libertas* (Stuttgart, 1936), pp. 187-90.

[5] Cf., for example, Voltaire's protest against Pascal's injunction to love only God and not the creatures, in the twenty-fifth of his *Lettres philosophiques;* or Chateaubriand on Pascal and Rousseau in *Le Génie du Christianisme,* 3ème partie, livre 2, chap. 6.

[6] *Pensées et opuscules,* pp. 244-7.

[7] A. Rüstow has called my attention to the fact that the formulation, "to create a harmony between might and justice" is used by Solon, fr. 24, 15-17. Since the line occurs in Plutarch's *Life of Solon* (translated by Jacques Amyot), it may be assumed that Pascal was familiar with it.

[8] Unlike the above-mentioned combination of ideas derived from Montaigne and Port-Royal, this combination of *raison d'état* with Augustinianism was no doubt unconscious, for Pascal was scarcely acquainted with the political theorists of his time and certainly did not study them in detail.

"La Cour et La Ville"

[1] *Je rends au public ce qu'il m'a prêté* ("to the public I return what it has lent me"; introduction to *Les Caractères*) and *Il se trouve des maux dont chaque particulier gémit et qui deviennent néanmoins un bien public, quoique le public ne soit autre chose que tous les particuliers* ("There are evils that every individual bemoans and that nevertheless become a public benefit, although the public is nothing other than the sum of all individuals"; *Du Souverain et de la république,* Par. 7).

[2] Henri Estienne, *Apologie pour Hérodote* (1566; reprinted Paris, 1879), Vol. I., p. 35: *le public (j'enten la communauté des amateurs des lettres)* . . . ("the public [I mean the community of the lovers of letters]"). In other words, he finds it necessary to define the word in this sense. Montaigne still employs *"le peuple"* for this purpose (*Essai* III, 2, beginning). Cf. also Larivey after Lintilhac, *Histoire générale du théâtre français,* II, 352.

[3] *Lettre à Balzac.*

[4] After Parfaict, *Histoire du théâtre français,* Vol. III, p. 226.

[5] Additional early examples: Scudéry in Parfaict, IV, 442

(1629), in Corneille's dedication of *Médée* to Monsieur P. T. N. G. (1639), and in polemics over *Le Cid*.

[6] Throughout the century *le public* is sometimes identical with the second part of the combination *la cour et la ville*. Cf. Molière, *Le Malade imaginaire*, II, 6, where *les grands* are contrasted with the *public;* or Baillet, *Jugemens des savans* (1685), IV, 385: *[Britannicus] est maintenant de toutes ses pièces celle que la Cour et le Public revoient le plus volontiers* ("Of all his plays it is now *Britannicus* that the court and the public most delight to see").

[7] As F. Schalk's article informs me, it already occurs in Sully's *Mémoires* (Cf. *Volkstum und Kultur der Romanen*, VII, I).

[8] Preface to *Remarques sur la langue française*.

[9] Presumably before 1640. Cf. Corneille's letter to Pellisson (*Œuvres*, ed. Marty-Laveaux, X, p. 477).

[10] The expression and the view of society connected with it spread widely and were long-lived. In congratulating Karl Zelter on the engagement of his son, Goethe wrote on January 1, 1817: "Court and town approve the union, which will be the foundation of splendid social relations." See also Goethe's letter to Carus of October 10, 1824.

[11] *Nouveaux Essais de critique et d'histoire.*

[12] There is an anecdote that the King inspired the scene of the hunter in *Les Fâcheux*. (*Ménagiana*, III, 24; Grimarest, *Vie de Molière*, ed. Liseux, p. 22.)

[13] The *parterre* corresponds topographically, though not sociologically, to our orchestra; it was the cheapest part of the house and consisted entirely of standing room. We shall have more to say of it below.

[14] Cf. Boileau, *Réflexion première sur quelques passages de Longin.*

[15] Quoted from Michaut, *Les Luttes de Molière* (Paris, 1925), p. 49. See also Ménage's remarks in Parfaict, X, 395a, or *Ménagiana*, I, p. 144. Highly characteristic is the ironic declaration made by Saint-Evremond after reading *Tartuffe:* "I have just read Tartuffe; it is Molière's masterpiece; I do not see how they have managed to prevent its performance for so long; if I am saved, it is to him that I shall owe my salvation. Devotion is so reasonable in the mouth of Cléante that it makes me renounce

my whole philosophy. . . ." (From a letter to M. d'Hervart, quoted in P. Mélèse, *Le Théâtre et le public à Paris sous Louis XIV* [Paris, 1934], p. 332).

[16] Still, there is a certain political factor to be considered, namely the King's dislike of secret cliques, which tried to evade his influence.

[17] Thirty sous for special performances. For further detail see Despois, *Le Théâtre français sous Louis XIV* (Paris, 1874), pp. 105 ff.

[18] This was the state of affairs even in the last years of the *confrèrie de la passion*. Cf. Parfaict, op. cit., Vol. 3, pp. 224 ff., esp. p. 237, note a; and Eugène Rigal, *Alexandre Hardy* (Paris, 1889), Chap. 2.

[19] *Prologues tant sérieux que facétieux.* Bruscambille was a stage name; his real name was Deslauriers. I have not been able to lay hands on the book itself but only read excerpts in Parfaict, op. cit., IV, 138 ff.; in J.-A. Dulaure, *Histoire civile, physique et morale de Paris*, 3rd ed. (Paris, 1825), Vol. 6, pp. 86 ff.; and finally in Rigal, op. cit., p. 145. Cf. also Rigal's bibliography. Bruscambille's dialogues are interesting also in that they show the appearance of grotesque metaphor in the language of popular farce, e.g.: . . . *je vous conjure . . . de recevoir un clystère d'excuses aux intestins de votre mécontentement.* . . .

[20] Parfaict, op. cit., V, 50.

[21] Parfaict, VI, 131. Cf. Lyonnet, *Les Premières de Corneille* (Paris, 1923), pp. 94 ff. On the position of the musicians and singers, see Mélèse, op. cit., pp. 382 and 417.

[22] Parfaict, VI, 150. Cf. also the two *filous* in the scene from Dorimon's *Comédie de la comédie* (1661) in Parfaict, IX, 31. On the disorders of the sixties and seventies, cf. Moland, *Vie de Molière*, p. 230. On Molière's successful protest against the right of the *officiers de la Maison du Roi* to attend performances free of charge, and on the related disorders, see Parfaict, X, 94, note. A similar incident involving the ambassador of Savoy in 1700 is described in Mélèse, op. cit., p. 63. Other disorders and incidents, ibid., p. 215 ff.

[23] The reference is to the recently founded theater in the Hôtel Guénegaud, resulting from a merger of the Marais with the remnants of Molière's troupe.

[24] Samuel Chappuzeau, *Le Théâtre français,* ed. Monval (Paris, 1875), p. 147. The above-mentioned decrees are cited on p. 153.

[25] Reproduced in Mélèse, op. cit., p. 419.

[26] See above, p. 147.

[27] Letter of Racine to Boileau, August 8, 1687.

[28] *La Maison des jeux,* quoted in Parfaict, VI, 128 ff., also in Lyonnet, op. cit., pp. 92 ff. I have not seen the book itself; cf. the bibliographical indications in the table at the beginning of Rigal's book on Hardy (Paris, 1889).

[29] Parfaict, VIII, 391. On Regnard's respect for the *parterre,* cf. Mélèse, *Théâtre,* pp. 210 ff. and *Répertoire,* pp. 335 ff.

[30] La Fontaine, *Epîtres,* XII, ll. 11 ff. See also the rest of the *Epître* and Despois, *Le Théâtre français sous Louis XIV* (Paris, 1874), pp. 335 ff.

[31] *Muse historique* of July 21, 1660. Cf. Parfaict, VIII, 366. To be sure, it was part of the current repertory.

[32] Littré on the word *"parterre,"* after Marmontel, *Œuvres,* Vol. VI, p. 327.

[33] Parfaict, IX, 183.

[34] Cf. Michaud, *Les Débuts de Molière à Paris* (Paris, 1923), pp. 229 ff. A reprint of *Zélinde* may be found in *Molière und seine Bühne, Molière-Museum,* ed. Dr. H. Schweitzer, with introduction and notes by H. Fritsche (Wiesbaden, 1881), pp. 19-68.

[35] Parfaict, X, 430. Cf. also the passage from Guéret's *Parnasse réformé* (1669) quoted by Mélèse in *Théâtre,* p. 133. I have unfortunately not been able to lay hands on Champmeslé's one-act comedy, *La Rue Saint-Denis* (1669).

[36] However, a development in this direction had already set in. My edition of Furetière's dictionary (1727) has the following under *"bourgeois":* Les ouvriers appellent aussi bourgeois celui pour lequel ils travaillent. Examples: *Il faut servir le bourgeois. Le maçon, l'artisan tâchent toujours à tromper le bourgeois.*

[37] I owe these details to the investigations that M. Albert-Marie Schmidt was kind enough to carry out at my request. He reports among other things that the best-known lace establishment employed some fifty lace-makers from Bruges and Venice.

[38] Letter from Gilberte Périer in *Lettres, opuscules et mé-*

moires de Mme Périer et de Jacqueline . . . , ed. Faugère (1845), p. 83; reproduced in the little Brunschvicg edition of Pascal's *Pensées et opuscules,* p. 247.

[39] Medium-priced places were also available: the benches on the inclined ramp behind the *parterre (amphithéâtre)* seem usually to have been occupied by the bourgeoisie, though they were sometimes reserved for princes of the royal family when they appeared with a large retinue. And there were also the upper *loges*. Concerning the prices and number of places in Molière's last theater, the rebuilt Palais Royal, cf. William Leonard Schwartz, "Molière's Theatre in 1672-1673," *Publications of the Modern Language Association,* LVI (1941), pp. 395 ff.

[40] See Rousseau, *La Nouvelle Héloïse,* Part II, letter 17.

[41] *Œuvres,* ed. Marty-Laveaux, Vol. V, p. 11.

[42] *Œuvres,* Vol. VI, p. 126. Corneille did not accept this tendency of his time entirely without resistance. In *Le Cid* Don Diègue appears, at least for a moment, as a broken old man. Cf. also Attila's nosebleed, of which he dies.

[43] Cf. Saint-Evremond's letter to the Comte d'Olonne, undated but definitely written in the late 1650's, in *Œuvres mêlées* (Amsterdam, 1706), Vol. I, p. 118, reprinted in Lanson, *Choix de lettres du 17e siècle* (Paris, 1913), p. 448.

[44] The term is modern—in those days it was called *ruelle, alcôve, réduit, cercle, cabinet*—while *salon* had the Italian meaning of a large, sumptuous hall.

[45] Tallement des Réaux, *Historiettes,* ed. Monmerqué, Vol. III, p. 214.

[46] As the century advanced the economic support of art fell more and more exclusively to the King and *le public*—but the King was the state, on whose protection *all* classes and professions depended.

[47] Madame de Rambouillet is quoted as having used the first phrase, Tallement, op. cit., p. 215; the second phrase is to be found in Jean de Balzac, *Lettres familières à M. de Chapelain* (Leiden, 1656), p. 105: . . . *puisque j'entre dans la confidence de Lucrèce, d'Horace et des autres honnestes gens de l'antiquité. . . .* The Latin *honestus* was used in the same sense in the imperial age (in Petronius or Seneca, for example).

[48] *Mémoires,* for 1699. Cf. Pascal, *Pensées,* 38 (ed. Brunschvicg). Of interest in connection with Racine are also the remarks of Spanheim, ambassador from Brandenburg (*Relation de la cour de Louis XIV en 1690* [Paris, 1900], reproduced in Mélèse, *Théâtre,* p. 85).

[49] Here we have no need to speak of the petty nobility, largely impoverished and living permanently in the provinces. Cf. the first chapters of Taine's *L'Ancien Régime.* A picture of social life in the provinces may be found in Molière's delightful *La Comtesse d'Escarbagnas.*

[50] As far as I know, La Bruyère is the only author who occasionally reveals an awareness of this.

[51] *Mémoires pour servir à l'histoire des hommes illustres de la république des lettres* . . . (Paris, 1727-45), 43 vol. The rest of our data are taken either from individual biographies or from the large French biographical collections of Michaud and Hoefer (*Biographie universelle* and *Nouvelle Biographie universelle*).

[52] This is a very approximate summary of a highly complex and confusing development. Cf. Holtzmann, *Französische Verfassungsgeschichte* (Munich, 1910) (Below-Meinecke, *Handbuch der mittelalterlichen und neueren Geschichte,* Vol. III, 4) and Paul Viollet, *Droit public,* Vol. IV: *Le Roi et ses ministres* (Paris, 1912).

[53] Richelieu wrote in his *Testament politique* (Chap. IV, Section 1): "In a newly established republic it would be a grave mistake not to do away with venality, because in such a case reason demands the institution of the most perfect laws that human society can endure. But prudence forbids the same policy in an old monarchy, whose imperfections have become a habit and whose disorder (not without utility) forms a part of the state order."

[54] Cf. Méré's remarks to the effect that *métier* and *honnêteté* were irreconcilable opposites (cf. Pascal, *Pensées et opuscules,* small Brunschvicg edition, 116). The "naturalness" of the *honnête homme* consisted precisely in his ability to be everywhere at his ease.

[55] See Charles Normand, *La Bourgeoisie française au 17e siècle* (Paris, 1908).

[56] *Le Misanthrope* takes place in court society—and the family

of Orgon in *Tartuffe* must belong either to the nobility or to the highest categories of the bourgeoisie.

⁵⁷ An *honnête homme* must not try to rise above his rank and above all he must not try to be original. In so early a work as *L'Astrée*, Part I, Book X (Bibliotheca Romanica edition, pp. 560-1), we read: *L'ambition que chacun doit avoir est de bien faire tout ce qu'il doit faire et en cela être le premier de sa condition. . . . Toutes choses devant se contenir dans les termes où la nature les a mises; et comme il n'y a pas apparence qu'un rubis pour beau et parfait qu'il soit puisse devenir un diamant, ainsi celui qui espère de s'élever plus haut, ou pour mieux dire de changer de nature et se rendre autre chose qu'il était, perd en vain le temps et la peine. . . .* ("It should be every man's ambition to do well what he is called upon to do and therein to be the first of his calling. . . . Since all things should remain within the limits appointed them by nature; and since it does not seem likely that a ruby, however perfect and beautiful it may be, can ever become a diamond, so he who hopes to raise himself higher or, more precisely, to change his nature and make himself something other than what he was, is wasting his time and trouble. . . .")

⁵⁸ *Essais*, II, 4.

⁵⁹ *1. Un marchand du Palais, ou un petit commis, sergent ou solliciteur de procez; 2. un marchand de soye, drappier, mouleur de bois, procureur du Chastelet, maître d'hôtel et secrétaire de grand seigneur; 3. un procureur en Parlement, huissier, notaire ou greffier; 4. un avocat, conseiller du Trésor ou des Eaues et Forests, substitut du Parquet et général des Monnoyes; 5. un auditeur des Comptes, trésorier de France ou payeur des Rentes; 6. un conseiller de la cour des Aydes ou conseiller du Grand Conseil; 7. un conseiller au Parlement ou un maistre des Comptes; 8. un maistre des Requestes, intendant des Finances, greffier et secrétaire du Conseil, président aux Enquestes; 9. un président au Mortier, vray marquis, sur-intendant, duc et pair.*

Vico and Aesthetic Historism

¹ Robert T. Clark, Jr., "Herder, Vico and Cesarotti," *Studies in Philology*, XLIV (1947), 645-71.

[2] *The Autobiography of Giambattista Vico,* translated from the Italian by Max Harold Fisch and Thomas Goddard Bergin (Ithaca, 1944), p. 64.

[3] This survey of the first two periods of Vico's *storia ideale eterna* is very incomplete; and for the purpose of this paper, the further development of the third period and the *ricorso delle cose umane* (the theory of the historical cycles) are not necessary. The best sources of information for the English reader interested in Vico's philosophy are the translation of Benedetto Croce's monograph (*The Philosophy of Giambattista Vico* [New York, 1913]) and Professor Fisch's introduction to the autobiography, quoted in our note 2. The first English translation of the *Scienza Nuova* (also by Bergin and Fisch, Ithaca, 1948) is an admirable achievement of a very difficult task.

[4] E.g., capoversi 246, 346, 347 of the two-volume Nicolini edition (Bari, 1928).

The Aesthetic Dignity of the "Fleurs du Mal"

[1] In E. Raynaud, *Charles Baudelaire* (Paris, 1922), p. 105, we find the following quotation from a play written in the 1840's:

> *Quel plaisir de tordre*
> *Nos bras amoureux,*
> *Et puis de nous mordre*
> *En hurlant tous deux.*

One is also reminded of Leconte de Lisle's poem about the wild dogs, *"Les Hurleurs."*

[2] *Sum levis, et mecum levis est, mea cura, Cupido,* says Ovid, *Amores,* 3, 1, 41. But all that is finished since Baudelaire; light love in poetry has become *Kitsch* or pornography. As late as the eighteenth century, in Chaulieu or Voltaire, for example, it was very different. In this connection it is interesting to read Baudelaire's instructions to his lawyer when *Les Fleurs du mal* was prosecuted for immorality; they may be found in a number of critical editions and biographies. He stresses the serious character of his poetry over against the *polissonnerie* of some of the "light" poems of Béranger and Musset, at which the authorities had taken no umbrage. We need only read these

poems to see how incredibly vulgar this erotic poetry in the "light style" had become.

³ Even in prose such matters were seldom treated. A few mild allusions occur in Montaigne. Crépet, in his critical edition (Charles Baudelaire, *Les Fleurs du mal: Edition critique établie par* Jacques Crépet *et* Georges Blin [Paris, 1942], p. 431; cited in the following as FdM, Crépet-Blin), expresses the belief that Baudelaire had read these passages in Montaigne and refers to *Essais*, II, Chap. XV. This is perfectly possible, but it is certain that Baudelaire learned nothing from Montaigne.

⁴ *"Semper eadem," "Tout entière," "Que diras-tu," "Le Flam-beau vivant," "A celle qui est trop gaie," "Réversibilité," "Con-fession," "L'Aube spirituelle," "Harmonie du soir," "Le Flacon," "Hymne."*

⁵ Baudelaire made many such statements. One of the most characteristic occurs in a letter to Fernand Desnoyers. It has often been cited, e.g., in FdM, Crépet-Blin, p. 463.

⁶ The tender, beautiful *"Je n'ai pas oublié"* refers to a happy period in his early youth, spent with his mother before her second marriage. Apart from this, wherever we find a gentler, more tender sentiment in *Les Fleurs du mal,* it usually proves to be deceptive. It is genuine when, in speaking to the beloved, he argues flight, renunciation, repose, or a numbing of the senses; then we find phrases such as *Mon enfant, ma sœur,* or *O ma si blanche, ô ma si froide Marguerite.*

⁷ Jean Royère (*Poèmes d'amour de Baudelaire* [Paris, 1927]) calls these breaches of style *catachrèses,* and gives an excellent description of them. Royère regards Baudelaire as a Catholic mystic; on the lines from *"Hymne à la Beauté"* of which we have quoted a part (*L'Amoureux pantelant . . .*) he writes (p. 123): "I decline to comment more directly on such verses. I content myself with reciting them every day like a Pater and an Ave." There are many such exaggerations in his book and almost all his ideas strike me as arbitrary and dilettantish. But even so it is a beautiful book.

⁸ This line is a good example of the romantic three-part alexandrine, with a caesura not after the sixth, but after the fourth and eighth syllables. It should be read and savored accordingly.

[9] There is a passage in which even *le Néant* does not seem to be nothing enough for him. It occurs in the *Projets de préface pour une édition nouvelle,* toward the end in the paragraph beginning with the words *D'ailleurs, telle n'est pas . . .* (FdM, Crépet-Blin, p. 214).

[10] Cf. the lines to Mme Sabatier (*Ta chair spirituelle a le parfum des anges*); or the following from "*Sonnet d'automne*":

> *. . . Mon cœur, que tout irrite,*
> *Excepté la candeur de l'antique animal*

"*J'aime le souvenir des ces époques nues*" is another example of this, although the apotheosis of youth at the end (*A la sainte jeunesse . . .*) is very startling in Baudelaire. Cf. the note in FdM, Crépet-Blin, p. 303.

[11] Royère, loc. cit., p. 58, writes: *Baudelaire . . . ne serait peut-être pas éloigné d'une théologie qui mettrait l'homme, en quelque manière, au niveau de Dieu.* But that would be the Devil's own theology. In this passage, to be sure, Royère is speaking more of the male than of humankind, but that scarcely makes a difference.

[12] *Ames choisies* is from the *Mémoires* of Saint-Simon, but may have been used earlier in the seventeenth century. The principle of selection has changed since then.

[13] Charles Baudelaire, *Ecrits intimes;* introduction by Jean-Paul Sartre (Paris, 1946).

[14] His hatred of nature often sounds Christian (*la femme est naturelle, c'est-à-dire abominable;* or *le commerce est naturel, donc il est infâme:* both from "*Mon cœur mis à nu*"). But it is so absurdly exaggerated (*j'aime mieux une boîte à musique qu'un rossignol,* as he is quoted as saying in Schaunard's *Souvenirs*), that it all seems to boil down to revolt. On the Apocalypse as the source of his visions of landscapes without vegetation (e.g., "*Rêve parisien,*" cf. Apoc. 21-2) see J. Pommier, *La Mystique de Baudelaire* (Paris, 1932), p. 39.

[15] The first version, which appeared in 1851 in *Le Messager de l'Assemblée,* is quite different, much weaker and milder; in the 1857 edition of *Les Fleurs du mal* the poem already has its definitive form, with the exception of the third line which runs: *Pour piquer dans le but, mystique quadrature . . .*

[16] Crépet (FdM, Crépet-Blin, p. 518) calls *"La Mort des artistes" la plus mallarméenne peut-être des Fleurs du mal*. This is incontestable. But perhaps one may equally well say that there is no better indication of the profoundly different character of the two poets.

[17] *Un état d'esprit auquel Baudelaire aura cessé de correspondre,* says E. Raynaud, loc. cit., p. 307.

[18] Like Taine after him, he called Baudelaire's style *âpre,* and wrote: *Vous chantez la chair sans l'aimer.* Aside from Ange Pechméja's letter, this is no doubt the most outstanding of contemporary judgments; J. J. Weiss should be mentioned as one of the contemporary adversaries. These and other critical remarks may be found in Eugène Crépet, *Charles Baudelaire: Etude biographique, revue et mise à jour par* Jacques Crépet (Paris, 1906), Flaubert, p. 359; Pechméja's letter, p. 414; Taine, p. 432. But the action against *Les Fleurs du mal* and the contemporary reaction to the book are treated at length in the other biographies. The most complete compilation of opinions is probably that of Vergniol in *La Revue de Paris,* August 1917.

MERIDIAN BOOKS

12 East 22 Street, New York 10, New York

Titles listed here are not necessarily available in the British Empire

LIVING AGE BOOKS

published by MERIDIAN BOOKS, INC.

12 East 22 Street, New York 10, New York

Titles listed here are not necessarily available in the British Empire

MERIDIAN BOOKS

12 East 22 Street, New York 10, New York

MERIDIAN GIANTS

MERIDIAN LIBRARY